JOHN MACQUARRIE

The Faith of the People of God

A Lay Theology

SCM PRESS LTD

334 00457 8

First published 1972
by SCM Press Ltd
58 Bloomsbury Street London WC1
Third impression 1978

Printed in Great Britain by
Fletcher & Son Ltd, Norwich

The Faith of the People of God

Contents

Preface

During most of my time as a teacher of theology, I have given courses not only for university students but for lay people, and have always found this a rewarding experience. This book could not have been written but for the contacts and discussions with my lay students. They have had a larger share in it than they know, and I gratefully dedicate it to them.

As lay people are being called upon to play an ever-increasing role in the life of the church, it is important that better provisions should be made for their theological training. But it is also important to understand that lay theology is not a simplified or watered down version of academic theology, but a distinct theological *genre*, with a character and dignity of its own.

Parts of this book originated in two lecture courses: the Mc-Math Lectures in the Diocese of Michigan on 'Christian Faith in the World Today', and the Prideaux Lectures in the University of Exeter on 'A Theology of the People of God'.

Christ Church, Oxford

I

Theology and the People of God

Lay theology is simply a special way of approaching the subject of theology. Thus, before we say anything about this special approach, we must consider what is theology in general. We begin from the fact that Christianity is a total way of life, and one could say the same about Judaism, Islam, Buddhism or any other of the major faiths of mankind. Such a way of life has many aspects. It implies beliefs about man and the world; it involves its adherents in the life of a community; it sets up a value system and urges some policies of action rather than others; it may encourage the practices of prayer, meditation, worship. This book is concerned mainly with the beliefs of Christianity, and it is important at the beginning that we should bear in mind that these beliefs, like the beliefs of the other faiths mentioned, are closely related to life and action. They are not airy speculations but convictions that have been worked out among men struggling to find a basic orientation for their lives. On the other hand, the beliefs constitute an indispensable factor in the way of life, and one cannot intelligently engage in such a way of life without giving thought to the beliefs which it presupposes, and critically examining them.

Christian theology is the attempt to state as clearly as possible the beliefs or doctrines that belong to the Christian way of life. It seeks also to show how these doctrines cohere among themselves, and how they are compatible with all the other beliefs that we hold in the modern world. Thus theology operates in a certain tension. It is responsible to the community whose beliefs it seeks to elucidate, it takes its rise within that community and is itself part of the community's life style. Yet in its quest for a statement of beliefs that will be both internally and externally coherent, theology is also, like any science or intellectual discipline, responsible to the demand for honest thinking. Sometimes there may be a conflict between loyalty to the beliefs of the community and commitment to intellectual integrity. Such a conflict may be resolved in various ways, for instance, by the revision of a traditional doctrine in the light of new knowledge. When this happens, theology exercises a critical function within the community, but this is still a function of the community itself. Theology is therefore at once the self-expression and the self-criticism of the community's beliefs. It follows that theology is not a static science. There is development of doctrine, as beliefs and their implications come to be better understood or as older formulations are revised in the light of new knowledge and criticism. The task of theology is never finished and there cannot be any final theology.

In seeking to show the compatibility of Christian doctrines with other beliefs about the world derived from secular disciplines and in many cases securely established, theology inevitably comes into relation with these disciplines. From the earliest times there has been a dialogue between theology and philosophy. From the philosophers, theologians have borrowed a great many terms which have then been employed for the articulation of theological statements; for instance, one may mention the important role played in patristic and medieval theology by the philosophical idea of 'substance'. Sometimes not only a terminology but an entire speculative content has been taken over; for instance, it has been claimed with some plausibility that the Christian theology of the early centuries adopted the Greek philosophical understanding of God, and superimposed this on the image of God arising from the Judaeo-Christian religious tradition. Some theologians have believed that these contacts with philosophy have led to the distortion of Christian doctrines, but others have held that it is only by the use of interpretative categories derived from philosophy that doctrines can be brought out of the religious ghetto and made intelligible to a wider public, so that their truth claims may be judged. It seems unlikely that theology could ever become entirely divorced from philosophy, and in any case this would be undesirable. In our own time theology develops through exchanges with such contemporary philosophical movements as existentialism, phenomenology, process philosophy, logical analysis and others.

Equally important have been the contacts between theology and history. Christianity is an historical religion and it makes some assertions concerning historical events, for instance, that Jesus Christ 'suffered under Pontius Pilate, was crucified, dead and buried'. Modern theologians have accepted that the historical affirmations of Christian faith must be investigated with all the rigour of historical method, and the result has been a far-reaching criticism of these affirmations, leading to a profoundly changed attitude toward the Bible and the tradition. The impact of history upon theology can scarcely be overestimated.

Theology has also had its points of contact with the empirical sciences. In the seventeenth century the new heliocentric astronomy provoked the famous clash between the church authorities and Galileo. In the nineteenth century came the equally famous conflict over Darwin's theory of evolution. These developments in science were held to conflict with the biblical doctrine of creation, but eventually the understanding of that doctrine was revised to take account of the new scientific knowledge. Theology must take cognizance of the interpretation of nature offered by the sciences and show the compatibility of this interpretation with theological pronouncements. Attention must be given also to those newer sciences, such as psychology and sociology, which have extended the methods of empirical science so far as possible to the nature of man and even to the phenomena of religion.

The issues mentioned in the last three paragraphs will all reappear later in the book. But it is already apparent that there are several possible types of theology, according as the theologian is preoccupied with the traditional doctrines themselves or with the task of relating them to the ideas that are prevalent in the culture of his time. A distinction has often been made between 'dogmatic' theology, charged with the task of setting forth in systematic fashion the accepted doctrines of the church, and 'apologetic' theology, concerned to come to grips with the presuppositions of secular culture and to show the relevance and truth of Christian doctrines in the face of that culture. The two types of theology have been well illustrated in recent times by the contrasting work of Barth and Tillich; the former stressed the theologian's responsibility to the tradition of faith, the latter saw his task primarily as that of bridging the gap between faith and secular culture. But the two types are not to be altogether separated. They are rather differences of emphasis (even when the difference is quite sharp) within the unitary work of theology. There can be no theological statement that remains unaffected by changing cultural conditions, no timeless expression of faith that speaks equally to every generation; on the other hand, a theology that is 'with it' in a cultural sense but has no roots in the tradition is not a Christian theology at all. In the present book, although we shall lean toward the apologetic rather than the dogmatic type of theology, we shall try not to let the obligation to address the contemporary world in terms intelligible to it obscure the equally valid obligation to speak out of the authentic Christian tradition.

This book is concerned with 'lay' theology. What is meant by this expression?

Perhaps I should begin by saying what is *not* meant by lay theology. It cannot be asserted too strongly that lay theology is not, so to speak, theology made easy, a simplified or abridged version of a 'professional' theology. Although in ordinary usage the word 'lay' is often contrasted with 'professional', it does not have that sense here. If we were correct in defining theology as 'the attempt to state as clearly as possible the beliefs or doctrines that belong to the Christian way of life',[1] then obviously theology is itself part of that way of life, for every intelligent Christian has an obligation to understand as clearly as he can the beliefs to which his faith has committed him. In other words, every intelligent Christian has an obligation to engage in theology. It is not the preserve of a professional class. Admittedly, the diversity of gifts within the Christian church means that always there are some people (usually clerics but sometimes laymen) who specially devote themselves to the study and teaching of theology. Admittedly, too, there has grown up an inflated theological jargon. But it is disastrous for the church when theology becomes a purely academic study and is divorced from the everyday life of the Christian community in the world. A lay theology might well dispense with some of the jargon, though theology will always need some technical words for accuracy of expression. But a lay theology is not an easy version

of an academic theology, and it would be an insult to the intelligence of the layman to suggest that it is. All theology
demands hard thinking. Lay theology is not a simplified version
of academic theology but rather a corrective to it, broadening
its base and bringing into being a theology that is more representative of the whole Christian community.

The word 'lay' is also contrasted with the word 'clerical'. But
a lay theology is *not* an anti-clerical theology. It means that
laity join with clergy in fashioning a theology commensurate
with the wider life of the church. Clerical theology tends to be
of the dogmatic type, a language spoken within the church to
the church, whereas we have indicated that lay theology will
lean toward the apologetic type,[2] a language addressed to the
world. For a long time, the church has been dominated by the
clergy, with the laity regarded almost as second-class citizens.
That state of affairs is changing. In the liturgical renewals of
recent years, care has been taken to ensure that the laity have a
definite active role in the worship of the church along with the
clergy – this is *concelebration* in the broad sense. In the reforms
of church government likewise, a larger voice has been given to
the laity – this is the principle of *collegiality*, again in a broad
sense. But if these reforms are to be meaningful, the laity must
also have a voice in the development of the church's doctrine –
there must be *cotheologizing*, if I may coin a word. There has
indeed been some recognition of the need for lay theological
education and some provision for it, but the foregoing remarks
will have made it clear that if the laity are to play in the church
the new responsible role that is being assigned to them, they
need not only training in theology but a voice in its formation.

In saying what 'lay theology' does *not* mean, I have made it
fairly clear what it does mean. I am taking the word 'lay' not in
the negative senses of 'non-professional' or 'non-clerical', but in
the affirmative sense of 'belonging to the people'. The English
word 'lay' is derived from the Greek noun, *laos*, 'people'. This
Greek word is used in the New Testament for 'the people of
God',[3] one of the most pregnant descriptions of the Christian
community. Lay theology, then, is a theology belonging to the
whole people of God, the laity as well as the clergy. If I may be
permitted to adapt some famous words of Lincoln, lay theology

is theology of the people of God, by the people of God, for the people of God.

To describe lay theology as a theology *of* the people of God is to choose for this theology a starting-point that will determine its whole shape and character. Since the doctrines of Christian faith all cohere and mutually imply one another,[4] it is possible to begin one's theological reflection from any doctrine and to proceed from there into the others. One may begin, for instance, from the word of God (Barth) or from the religious self-consciousness of man (Schleiermacher) or from the concept of justification (Ritschl), but to reflect on any one of these matters in any depth leads into a consideration of the whole spectrum of Christian doctrines. But the starting-point establishes a perspective from which the whole is seen, and the very different types of theology that we find in Barth, Schleiermacher and Ritschl (to mention only the three theologians named above) shows how influential the choice of starting-point is. We have chosen as the starting-point for our lay theology the people of God. This is the fundamental datum from which our inquiry sets out. There are some obvious advantages in beginning this way. For instance, our initial datum, the people of God, is a fact the existence of which cannot be doubted, a real phenomenon of the world. We do not have to begin by trying to prove the existence of God or establishing the historical reality of Christ, though to be sure we shall not seek to evade such questions as the argument proceeds. We begin with an indisputable fact that would demand explanation in any case – that there is a worldwide community claiming to be the people of God and confessing that it owes its existence to Jesus Christ. If God and Christ seem to be questionable realities, at least we cannot question the reality of the Christian community, which is itself the principal testimony to the reality of Christ and the God revealed in him. As John Knox has written, 'the only difference between the world as it was just after the event (of Jesus Christ) and the world as it had been just before is that the Church was now in existence'.[5] It is this new phenomenon, this people of God, into which we must inquire, asking about its origin, history and destiny; its relation to the whole human race; its faith and inner life; its structure and mission. Our starting-point will have the further advantages of keeping before us the corporate nature of Christian faith and the context of that faith in the life and action of people set in the world, but this can be shown only as we go along.

Lay theology, we have said, is not only of the people, it is *by* the people. This does not mean that every member of the people of God writes theology, though we have seen that every intelligent Christian has a duty to think out the meaning of his faith, and thus to think theologically. It is not meant, either, that lay theology must be written by laymen, though in fact there have been many excellent lay theologians and probably their number will increase in the future. What is meant by saying that lay theology is a theology by the people is that such a theology must bring to expression the life of the people as engaged in the tasks of the world. It will avoid the clericalism which has sometimes shut up theology within the ecclesiastical world, and it will likewise avoid the professionalism which has sometimes turned theology into an abstruse scholastic refining of distinctions having little relevance to the life of the people. Although lay theology will be produced by individuals, some of whom may even be clerics, they can claim to be producing lay theology only to the extent that they participate in the life of the people of God and are open to the many currents flowing through it. They try to let themselves be spokesmen for the community in the life of which they participate, though this does not exclude a prophetic function which may sometimes bring them into collision with opinions prevalent in the community. Nevertheless, it is in this kind of cotheologizing rather than from a sheltered specialized approach that the meaning of the Christian doctrine in the breadth of its application to the life of man is to be reached. A parallel may be seen in the experiment of the 'shared sermon' in which members of the congregation are invited to make their contributions toward the interpretation of the text. Though the result is sometimes confused, the procedure can open up in a remarkable way the range of meaning in the text and may reveal in a salutary way to the clerical preacher (as it has done to the present writer!) how remote the interests governing his own interpretation are from those of many of his lay brethren in the church.

Our third point was that a lay theology is a theology *for* the people. It cannot be stressed too much that the people of God is a *people*, not just an assembly or a crowd, and still less a mob. A people has a certain unity, and one important strand in that unity is a self-understanding. The people knows its identity, and has formed an idea of its nature, role and purpose. Only so can it be a real force in human affairs. It is strange that so many Christians think that theology is some kind of luxury which they can leave to the specialists or those who happen to like it. No doubt this tells us something about the remoteness of much traditional theology. But theology, properly understood, is no luxury. It is a necessity if there is to be a true people of God. Theology is the people's understanding of its own *raison d'être*, and without such an understanding, there is not a people but only an uncertain, drifting, spineless mass of human beings. If the church sometimes appears to be such a jellylike mass, one reason for this (though not the only reason) is the lack of any clear theological understanding. To supply this understanding is the business of a theology for the people, a theology which will not be the specialized preserve of scholars and professionals but which will relate to the interests and life situations of the great bulk of mature and intelligent Christians. All theology is addressed to someone, consciously or unconsciously. Much theology has been addressed by specialists in the academic world to other specialists like them. There is indeed a place for this type of theology, but there has been too much neglect in building up the whole people in theological understanding.

We may now sum up the introductory remarks of this first chapter. Christian theology is the attempt to make clear the beliefs implicit in the Christian way of life. It is rooted in that life itself, but, as a reflective discipline, it also stands in relation to philosophy, the sciences and the culture generally. Lay theology is particularly concerned to relate the theological enterprise to the whole people of God. It is theology of the people, by the people, for the people. Its approach to theology is therefore guided by the idea of the people of God, and it is to the exploration of this idea that we now turn.

Notes

1. See above, p.1.
2. See above, p.3.
3. I Peter 2.10.
4. See above, p.1.
5. John Knox, *The Early Church and the Coming Great Church*, London: Epworth Press, 1957, p.45.

II

The People as Primary Theological Datum

We have seen that the starting-point of our lay theology is the fact of the existence of a community claiming to be the people of God and of Christ.[1] This fact constitutes the primary theological datum. In the third century of our era, Origen wrote: 'Something new has happened since the time when Jesus suffered ... the massive rise of the Christian people, as if suddenly brought forth.'[2] Admittedly, in the twentieth century the existence of this people may strike us as a fact less impressive and less dramatic than it seemed to Origen. The novelty has long ago worn off and the failures of the community itself have cheated many of the early expectations. Yet the continuing existence of the community through the centuries in the face of outward attack and inward collapse is itself a phenomenon that calls for explanation. And even today, familiarity has not entirely obscured the fact that something new is striving for expression in this community, a new form of humanity. This community, then, constitutes the material for our theological questioning, analysis, interpretation. Who is this people? What is its faith? What is its self-understanding? What can we learn of its origin and destiny, and of the deep springs of its life? What can possibly be meant by calling any community the people of God?

In this chapter we shall attempt only a preliminary exploration of our datum. Naturally we shall concentrate attention on what is new in this community, on the unique features which distinguish the people of God from all the other peoples and communities of the human race. But even at this stage we shall

soon see that the people of God has, so to speak, blurred edges.
Its boundaries cannot be strictly demarcated. It flows over into
other communities and indeed has affinity with the whole
human race.

Let us begin by asking what it is that gives to a company of
human beings the cohesion and solidarity that constitute them
a 'community' or 'people'. There is no single answer to this
question, for there are many kinds of communities, peoples,
associations. Sociologists have often made the distinction between groups in which the bond is natural, and those in which
it is conventional. In the traditional sense of the word, a people
is a natural community. It is most commonly bound together
by the kinship of race or clan, and even today this kind of bond
evinces itself in powerful feelings of racial and national consciousness. But the bond of the people of God is entirely
different. From the beginning, this was a people embracing
'Jew and Greek and barbarian',[3] and it was precisely this trans-
racial and transnational character of the people that was so
deeply impressive in the early centuries and that seemed like
the advent of a new humanity. In spite of some local lapses, the
people of God has continued to establish community across
the natural boundaries of race, nation and clan, and rightly
sees this as one of its major tasks today. Another natural bond
is language, which sometimes unites in one people different
ethnic groups. The importance of language for a people is
recognized in the myth of the tower of Babel, according to
which the unity of mankind through a single primeval language gave way to division and strife when this was superseded
by many languages.[4] Language can make both for unity and for
misunderstanding and division. But once more this natural
bond is not characteristic of the people of God. With the Babel
story in the Old Testament one may contrast the Pentecost
story in the New Testament, which tells not of the reversal of
Babel but of how in the new community those who spoke different languages became intelligible to each other.[5] The cohesion
of the people of God does not depend on the abolition of
natural differences, but gathers them up and preserves them in
a richer diversity-in-unity than can be found in any natural
community. When we turn from natural bonds of union to
those that are conventional, we still do not find anything that

sheds light on the bond that holds together the people of God. For these conventional bonds are based on a shared interest – it may be security or commerce or even benevolence. But the point about the people of God is that it brings into one community those who have no shared interests of the kind mentioned, and even those whose interests are antithetical. Not only Jew and Greek and barbarian, but free man and slave, came together in the new people.[6]

The bond which holds together the people of God and constitutes them a community is different from anything like race, language or common interest. The bond is faith, and the people of God can be described as fundamentally a community of faith.

It is unfortunate that faith has frequently been equated with belief, and the church has encouraged this misconception by laying an undue emphasis on correctness of belief and making this the primary criterion of its membership. Obviously, belief is not unimportant, and if a person's beliefs are erroneous, his conduct may be profoundly distorted. But faith is something more inclusive than belief. It is a total attitude toward life, and although belief is a part of this attitude, its essence is to be seen rather in commitment to a way of life. It may be the case that when the commitment is made, all the beliefs implied in it are not yet clear, and it is only in following out the commitment that the beliefs come to be fully and explicitly understood. This is true not only of the individual coming into the community, but of the community itself. The Christian community began with a commitment to Jesus Christ, but it took some centuries to work out the basic beliefs that were already implicit in the act of commitment, and the unfolding of these beliefs still continues.

The structure of faith may be described as fourfold. First, there is the basic element of commitment, already mentioned. The community of faith has decided for one way of life in preference to other possible ways. This fundamental attitude of commitment implies loyalty, obedience, attachment, trust toward certain ends and values, defined in the case of the Christian community in terms of Jesus Christ. Second, the kind of commitment about which it is appropriate to use the language of faith is not just one commitment among others. It is, to use Paul

Tillich's expression, an 'ultimate concern'.[7] This is not another
concern added on to our day-to-day concerns, but the over-
arching criterion by which we assign priorities among our
ordinary concerns so that they show some unitary consistency
and directedness. The ultimacy of the faith commitment finds
expression in such language as the confession that Christ is
Lord or the Son of God. Third, commitment to an ultimate
concern involves the acceptance of some beliefs, though, as we
have noted, these may not be entirely clear at the time. But,
as rational beings, we are bound sooner or later to reflect on
the grounds of our commitment. An unreflecting commitment
can easily degenerate into mere fanaticism. A commitment to
Jesus Christ implies at the very least the beliefs that he is a
real person and a significant person; an *ultimate* commitment
to him would seem to imply considerably more. Though faith
is not primarily belief, it cannot be reduced to a purely practical
matter, and it leads inevitably into theological questions. Fourth,
faith is always experienced as response. It is not something that
we create for ourselves. Faith is awakened in us by a reality outside of ourselves claiming the allegiance of that which is most
deeply within ourselves. The people of God did not generate
itself, but came into being in response to the reality which was
manifesting itself in Jesus Christ. Thus the community of faith
understands itself as owing its existence to a prior act of revelation.

Especially in a scientific age, the idea of revelation is trouble-
some for many people. Must not all knowledge be won by
skill and ingenuity and mental effort? How, then, can there be
revelation, or how could anything so dubious as a revealed
knowledge be entitled to respect alongside the kind of knowledge that has been established by recognized procedures of
investigation? The misunderstanding which underlies such
questions is similar to the misunderstanding of faith as belief.
Just as faith is more than belief, so revelation is more than
knowledge. If we think of Jesus Christ as the revelation which
called into being the Christian community of faith, then obviously he was not a body of knowledge. He was a living person,
and although one can say many things about a living person,
one can never reduce him to a series of statements. As a person,
Christ made a total impact on the first Christians – on their

standards of value, their policies of action, their wills and emotions, just as much as on their minds. He was revelation not in the sense that he imparted a secret knowledge[8] to them but because, just by being the person he was, he extended their vision of what it means to be a human being, he caused them to see the world in a new light and to have a new insight into the mystery of God. The revelation created first commitment, and only secondarily and on reflection knowledge.

In our ordinary experience we can find parallels which help to throw light on the nature of revelation. Getting to know another person, for instance, is not something that we accomplish by our own unaided efforts; it requires his gift, his self-revelation. But we can hardly have an experience of this kind without having our horizons expanded. Another case is the experience of being seized by a great work of art. It presents us with a new way of seeing things, and this too comes to us as a gift. It is notoriously difficult in both the cases mentioned to put what is received into words, for it impinges on the whole personal being. Still more difficult is it to put into words revelation in its theological sense, for in this case something ultimate has grasped a whole community in every dimension of its being.

The idea of revelation has been very prominent in modern theology, but because this idea has been so often understood in the narrow sense of conveying new knowledge rather than in the sense of opening up new life, there might be some advantage in using an alternative term that will better express the inclusive sense intended. The theological vocabulary does in fact supply such a term: 'grace'. The Christian community confessed: 'Grace and truth came through Jesus Christ.'[9] Faith can be described as the response to grace just as well as the response to revelation, and the language of grace points not only to the gift-like character of that which evokes faith but to the fact that it impinges on and enhances every area of life – that it brings into being a new human community, the people of God.

Some such creative event, the awakening of faith through an overwhelming experience of grace or revelation, must be posited at the beginning of that community, the people of God, which still confronts us today as a given fact in the world. The community's own testimony is that this grace came through Jesus Christ. But how can a community today still live in the strength of a revelation or act of grace that occurred about two thousand years ago? At this point we must take into account another factor that is of the greatest importance in constituting any people or community, namely, history. A people learns its identity, deepens its character and enhances its solidarity through a history. This is true of the great nations of the world – the Americans, the British, the Russians all bring with them a history which continues to shape their present attitudes. The history is not simply a plain record of facts, but an interpreted record related to the ideals and values of the people in question. There could not be a people without a history, for a history confers meaning, identity and dignity. Thus it is never just something from the past, but is a present possession and a hope for the future. It is interesting to note how as black Americans have developed a sense of national consciousness, they have at the same time revived the study of black history. Though a broad ocean and several centuries of oppression separate them from the medieval kingdoms of Africa, they have found in the history of these old African cultures a source of identity and dignity. History does for a people what memory does for an individual. Without memory, no one could have an identity, no one could have the dignity of being a person or have hope for the future.

It is exactly so with the people of God. It has cherished in its collective memory the great creative moments in which it came into existence, and this memory of its history has sustained it through many adversities. Yet the word 'memory' is hardly adequate in this context. It is not simply the memory of a great creative beginning in the past that has sustained the identity of the people. It is rather that the revelation and grace that were present at the beginning can be recalled in such a way that they are present again as revelation and grace, evoking again and again the response of faith. Indeed, if there is any proof of the truth or adequacy of a revelation, it must be something like this – that the people can turn to it again and again and still find it revelation, in the sense that it still lights up the meaning of human existence in the world and still pushes back the horizons of this existence.

The continuing living presence of the initial revelation in the community of faith has been ensured by two means – scripture and tradition. These two complement one another. Scripture, in isolation from the ongoing life and developing thought of the community, would be a dead record of the past; on the other hand, the developing life and thought of the people needs both the control and the inspiration which scripture supplies.

The scriptures of the New Testament have a unique importance and authority because they embody the earliest testimony of the people to those experiences of grace and revelation which had given it its existence as a people. That testimony may be summed up in words from the prologue to the Fourth Gospel: 'The Word became flesh and dwelt among us, full of grace and truth; we have beheld his glory, glory as of the only Son from the Father.'[10] The word 'glory' points to a depth of meaning in the experience as if it were a source of light, and this is what is meant by calling it 'revelation'. Historical criticism makes it appear very improbable that we actually have in the New Testament the testimony of eye-witnesses, as was long believed. Such criticism has also raised questions about the literal accuracy of the gospel narratives and the authenticity of some of the sayings attributed to Jesus. Later we shall have to face the implications of these findings of biblical scholarship.[11] But we can acknowledge at once that the idea of the Bible as an infallible book is a mistaken one. The New Testament did not fall ready made from the skies, but was penned by fallible members of the people of God, trying as best they could to find words that would express the glory, the grace and truth, that had called the people into existence. The rich and many-sided reality that had created the new community could not possibly be put entirely into words. What is astonishing is that the New Testament does bring the reality so vividly before us.

But I have said that scripture only comes alive in the life of the community. It is to this continuing life of the community that the word 'tradition' refers. The revelation itself was a personal life and could not therefore be completely transposed into words. As Gabriel Moran has said, 'Only with a personal life could one give something of an adequate testimony.'[12] The new life of the people of God, in all its fullness, was the most adequate testimony to the revelation. The life of the community was there before the New Testament was written. The community decided which of the many writings circulating in the early church should be included in the canon of the New Testament. On the basis of the New Testament, the community went on to new explorations of Christian truth and doctrine and to new applications of Christian ethics. This continues today. The New Testament remains as, so to speak, the written charter of the people. There could be no development of doctrine that was disloyal to this source. Yet subsequent generations of the people have been led into new understandings of Christian faith, no doubt implicit in the New Testament but not explicitly grasped by the writers themselves. If indeed the glory revealed in Christ is in any way commensurate with what Christians have claimed for it, then not only was it not fully grasped by the first generation of the people, there must also be unexhausted truths waiting to be discovered by the people of the present and of the future.

A political analogy will help to make these matters clearer. The constitution of the United States is the written document testifying to the fundamental principles on which the nation was created. It remains as a norm and a stabilizing force. But the full meaning of the document was not understood by the founding fathers. Only in the subsequent ongoing life of the people did its implications begin to appear. They are still appearing in the twentieth century and will continue to be discovered, as the constitution is interpreted in new ways to meet new needs and to ensure a better life for the citizens. The constitution, then, is not a static heritage from the past but, within the life of the community, is still a creative instrument.

In the people of God, scripture and tradition have through their interaction gradually built up the accepted body of Christian doctrine. On them have been based the catholic creeds, succinct statements of the essentials of Christian doctrine. On the other hand, some positions have been excluded, as conflicting either with scripture or with the consensus of opinion as to how scripture should be interpreted; these were the so-called 'heresies', the opinions of individuals or groups which failed to win the approval of the people as a whole and might even be felt as disruptive of the life of the community and a departure from the truth entrusted to it. Thus the people continues to live in the presence of that creative experience which gave it birth. Through the mediation of scripture and tradition, it continues to draw from its sources of grace and revelation; and while it remains loyal to its origin, and preserves its identity, it looks for new understandings of its faith and for new roles to play.

In this chapter we have made a preliminary analysis of the primary theological datum, the people of God, and we have seen how it is constituted by faith as response to revelation, and how it has maintained its identity by scripture and tradition. Much more remains to be said and many details have to be filled out. As the next step toward extending our view, let us remember that the people of God which came into being with the Christian revelation claimed to be the successor of an older people of God. As well as its own New Testament, the Christian community took over the Hebrew scriptures and called them the Old Testament. As said at the beginning of this chapter, the people of God has blurred edges and merges into other communities. The new people of God saw the essentials of its life already prefigured in that first people, and it is to that first people that we now turn in our theological inquiry.

Notes

1. See above, p.6.
2. Origen, *Contra Celsum*, VIII, 43. Origen uses the word *ethnos* rather than *laos* for 'people'.
3. Colossians 3.11.
4. Genesis 11.1-9.
5. Acts 2.1-12.
6. Colossians 3.11.
7. Paul Tillich, *Systematic Theology*, Welwyn: Nisbet, 1951-63, I, p.11.
8. The ancient Gnostics supposed that Jesus imparted a secret knowledge (gnosis) just as some sects today supposed that revelation consists in esoteric information about world events.
9. John 1.17.
10. John 1.14.
11. See below, pp.57ff.
12. Gabriel Moran, *Theology of Revelation*, London: Burns and Oates, 1967, p.81.

III

The First People of God

The primary datum of Christian theology is the Christian community itself, the people of God. But that people does not occur as an isolated phenomenon, for while it has its distinctive character, is has also many affinities with the other peoples who with it constitute the human race and its history. In particular, the Christian community has from the beginning recognized a special relation to the people of Israel, whom we may appropriately call the first people of God.

The origins of the first people of God are recounted in the stories concerning Abraham, the first man of faith. These stories, like the stories concerning the origin of any nation, even any modern nation, are no doubt compounded as much of idealistic imagining as of plain fact. Yet in a remarkable way these stories of the beginning already contain in themselves most of the essential characteristics that were later to unfold in the development of the community as a people of God.

Abraham probably lived about two thousand years before the Christian community came into existence. There has been some discussion as to whether Abraham was an individual or a tribe. In all likelihood, he was both. All human existence is corporate, and the individual is an abstraction. Abraham always has his companions, and the stories are concerned with the birth of a people rather than the career of an individual. Yet a people itself exists for the fulfilment of individuals, and it needs the vision and leadership of individuals. At a later time the Christian community was to form around Jesus Christ, but even he remains inseparable from those whom he called.

The stories about Abraham consist on the one hand of human incidents – journeys, settlements, family events, quarrels, the ordinary stuff of existence, so to speak. But interspersed through this is his dialogue with God, known as a personal power who may be encountered as an inner voice, or in a vision, or in a direct theophany. This divine power both promises and commands, and the everyday events in the life of the nascent community are interpreted in the light of the dialogue with God.

When the story begins, Abraham is living in the important commercial city of Haran in Mesopotamia. He hears the voice of the Lord: 'Go from your country and your kindred and your father's house to the land that I will show you. And I will make of you a great nation, and I will bless you and make your name great, so that you will be a blessing.'[1] In obedience to the call, Abraham and his companions go out. We recognize in this incident at the origin of the first people of God the same pattern that we have noted in the case of the Christian community. There is an experience of grace or revelation, an encounter with a compelling reality which the believer calls God; and there is the response of faith – in Abraham's case, a commitment to the Voice and a going out into an unknown land and an unknown future.

We notice further that the people is constituted by an act of separation. Abraham and his companions turn their backs on the secular cities of the Mesopotamian civilization. Since we hear a good deal nowadays about the need for the involvement of the people of God in the world, it is important that we should be clear that this is a more complicated matter than it is often represented to be. If the business of the people of God were simply to identify with secular society, then Abraham and his companions would never have left Haran at all. They would have lived on happily there, and we would never have heard of them or of this strange phenomenon, the people of God. But if the people is to do anything or be anything at all significant, it must have something distinctive about it. It is not a question of choosing between separation and involvement, but the much more difficult one of living in a tension between these two. The people of God lives in a dialectical relation with the world. Only if it is to some extent separated from the world can it help the world, but it is separated in order that it may help and not that it may live in isolation. Abraham is summoned out of Haran not only that he may be blessed but that he may be a blessing. As Louis Bouyer has said of Abraham and his companions, 'the particular destiny which is theirs reveals itself from the beginning as obscurely bound to the common destiny of all mankind'.[2] We shall see more of this in a moment.

But meanwhile we return to the stories about the beginnings of the people of God. It is surely not an accident that one of the first episodes tells of the people's sin.[3] They had separated themselves from the Mesopotamian city, but this did not mean that they were delivered from the sin which runs through all humanity. In the course of a famine, Abraham and his companions went down to Egypt. His wife being of great beauty, Abraham was afraid that the Egyptians might kill him to gain possession of her, so he passed her off as his sister. She was taken into the Pharaoh's harem. When the deception was discovered, the pagan Egyptians acted with more integrity than the people of God had shown. This self-critical episode makes it clear that the people of God is not infallible – indeed, it is only on the way to becoming the people of God in the full sense, and sometimes its moral discernment will not equal that of ordinary men and women who are also God's creatures, though not explicitly within the people. This reminds us again that the edges of the people are not sharply defined. Yet if the people is not infallible and is still subject to sin, it may claim to be indefectible, in the sense that God has promised it fullness of being in the future and will recall it from its wanderings and defections. Indeed, the whole story of the first people of God in the Old Testament is largely in the recurring pattern of falling away and return.

The next episode introduces a further ambiguity. It tells of the first division in the people of God.[4] Quarrels have broken out in the company. As a result, Lot and his followers hive off from Abraham's people. Traditionally, his descendants became the tribes of Moab and Ammon, rivals in later times of the people of Israel. Further divisions and separations occurred in the subsequent history of the people of God. Sometimes this has been regarded as a kind of refining process by which the people was cut down to the genuinely faithful remnant. This may be an oversimplified explanation, but the occurrence of these divisions and separations makes it plain that there is not a merely automatic succession or continuation of the people in history.

Sometimes the line was broader, sometimes narrower, but still the line continued toward the promised fulfilment.

We pass on to one of the most dramatic of the stories about Abraham and one in which we are again confronted with the dialectic of separation and involvement in the life of the people of God. Abraham, who had separated himself from the city of Haran, could have felt little attraction for the cities of the plain, Sodom and Gomorrah, noted even in those ancient times for the licentiousness of their life.[5] But when Abraham learns that they are to be destroyed, he intercedes for them. The people of God may be neither self-centred nor exclusive, and certainly not vindictive. It remains 'obscurely bound' to the common destiny of all mankind, and its separation does not mean opting out of the human race but rather seeking a point from which help may be given. The ties of solidarity even with the doomed cities of the plain are brought out in the story. For one thing, Lot and his people have gone to live there; for another, good and bad are mingled together, and is it not better that the bad should be saved with the good than the good destroyed with the bad? Abraham's eloquent intercession for the city shows us the dialectic of separation and involvement in the people in what we may call its priestly role. The people of God is also 'a royal priesthood'.[6] It has been called to this priesthood not for the sake of cultivating its own life but so that it may work and pray for the rest of mankind, as Abraham does in the incident we have considered.

One last story from the Abraham cycle must be mentioned. The command comes to him from that constraining Power that has governed his whole life: 'Sacrifice your son!'[7] How shattering this must have been! For the future of the people of God and all the promises that had been made seemed to be bound up with the son and heir, Isaac. There have been many interpretations of this story, and the original meaning remains obscure. I shall not attempt any detailed discussion, but simply say that at this early stage the idea of sacrifice is introduced into the account of the people. The gospel paradox that the man who seeks to save his life will lose it, while the man who is prepared to lose it will actually enhance it, is already foreshadowed in the matter of the projected sacrifice of Isaac, but in this case on the level of the entire people of God. For Isaac, the son who had come so late on the scene, had become the visible, tangible embodiment of the future of the people – he *was* the people, focusing all the promises to which it looked forward. But whenever (then or later) the people rested its hope and found its security in someone or something taken into possession within itself, its advance was halted, it was no longer moving into its future, it was losing its distinctive life and beginning to disintegrate; only when it was ready to transcend every situation and move out beyond in response to the constraining Power that it had known from the beginning, was it moving toward fulfilment. Every security that threatened to turn the people back into themselves must be itself threatened, and this is one way in which we might understand the perplexing story of Abraham and Isaac. We could express this in another way by saying that the people had to discover that their priestly role was a costly one – so costly that the people might have to become victim as well as priest.

We have spent some little time over these stories of the beginning of the first people of God because they are so pregnant with the whole future of that first people and also of the new people that followed it. The origin of anything great is itself great. However, history is needed for the development of peoplehood. Here we can only glance at some of the most significant moments in the history of the first people of God.

We pass over the centuries from Abraham to the events associated with Moses. These events were of decisive importance in the formation of the people. Though we have spoken of the people of God, we have not much explored so far what this qualification, 'of God', means. In the Moses stories, God shows himself more clearly, and we can better understand what is meant by a people *of God*. Three incidents are specially instructive.

The first is God's revelation of his name to Moses in the course of the theophany at the burning bush.[8] The God of Abraham, Isaac and Jacob had not made known his name to these patriarchs, but now he tells it to Moses: 'I am who I am.' There has been endless discussion over the meaning of these celebrated words, and at a later time an elaborate philosophical theology was built out of them. The name Yahweh, used by some of the Hebrew tribes for the deity, sounds very much like the Hebrew

verb meaning 'I am'. But the early Hebrews were an unphilo-
sophical race, and in interpreting the name of God as 'I am
who I am', they certainly did not mean anything so subtle as
that God is 'self-subsistent being', to use the expression of a
later age. Yet that later philosophy may claim to be a legitimate
development from the revelation of the divine name. In any
case, no intellectually convincing theology can sidestep the
philosophical question about the meaning and reality of God.
In calling God 'I am', the Hebrews were acknowledging that
the God of Abraham and Isaac and Jacob, the disturbing Power
that had brought them into existence as a people, is also the
fundamental reality. Whatever else one may say about God, one
must say that he is.[9] The Hebrew verb 'to be', however, had a
very dynamic sense. To speak of God in terms of being is not
to be understood in a static, timeless way. God is rather the
power of being, the very act of existing, the dynamic source that
lets be whatever is. The people of God, then, are the people who
acknowledge the invisible but dynamic mystery of God as the
ultimate reality.

If the first incident we have considered answers the question
'Who is God?' in terms of being, the next incident (or series of
incidents) takes up the question, 'What does God do?' We may
say that it answers it in terms of liberation. I am referring, of
course, to the story of the exodus from Egypt.[10] The Israelites
were enslaved and had virtually ceased to be a people. But
through Moses they hear again the voice of their God, summoning them to go out into the desert, as Abraham had done long
before. In a remarkable way which so impressed itself on the
memory of the people that they celebrate it to this day in the
Passover, the Israelites escaped from their oppressors, crossed
the Red Sea, and began a new existence. They believed that
these happenings had been made possible by the fact that
history is shaped not only by human decision but by God, whom
we might even describe as the power of history itself. I have
described this activity as liberation. This was not an easier life,
or a more pleasant life. The escaped Hebrews were in fact
tempted to regret the relative affluence of their life in Egypt.
Yet true humanity and dignity lies not in the production and
consumption of goods but in responsible freedom. God's liberation from Egypt set the pattern by which not only the Hebrew

people but many oppressed peoples since have looked for his action in history.

The third incident from the Mosaic period is the giving of the law in the desert and the new covenant relationship into which the people enter with their God.[11] This defines still more clearly what is meant by talk of 'God', and how God is experienced in human life. God is linked inseparably with the moral demand. To acknowledge God is to acknowledge the ultimacy of this demand. To make anything else more ultimate is the idolatry of setting up false gods before the one God. The God of the Old Testament, we should notice, is hardly a comforting, reassuring God, and is therefore unlikely to be a product of wishful thinking. Rather, while the idols promise ease and pleasure, the God Yahweh is disturbing and demanding. But the idols are deceptive and lead to the diminution and destruction of the humanity of the people, while God's demand leads them into a more genuine and mature humanity.

We must hasten on to a later phase in the story of that first people of God. Under David, the people had become a moderately strong nation, well established in its territory. Next a temple was built as the focus of that national life. To some it might have seemed that the promises given to Abraham were now being fulfilled. But all this was short-lived. The people was once again divided. And at last came the most crushing blow of all – the holy city of Jerusalem was captured, its temple destroyed, and the flower of the nation scattered in captivity. One might compare this blow to the hopes of the people to the threat to the life of Isaac long before, except that this time there was no restraint placed on the destroying hand.

We can only imagine what a traumatic event this must have been in the life of the people. It has been suggested that many of them probably lapsed into paganism at this time, believing that history had falsified the beliefs of the people of God. But there were some who survived even this catastrophic blow to their hopes and who were led by it to a deeper understanding of what it means to be the people of God. They remembered that for several centuries prophetic voices had been heard in Israel, reminding the people that God's favour was not automatic, that their election did not mean a life of ease and indulgence, and that idolatrous attachment to self-centred securi-

The First People of God 25

ties could only lead to destruction. We may say that this was the working out of the truths already hidden in that early story of the projected sacrifice of Isaac. It was not the end, but the recall of the people to their true destiny and their liberation from the false ideals which had come to dominate them. God had not forsaken them, but was calling them out of the dead end in which they had come to a halt.

Thus it was in the turbulence of the post-exilic times that the people of God came to have the noblest and profoundest understanding of its identity and destiny. It became clear at last that this special kind of peoplehood, founded on faith, was not bound to any natural community, to any nation or political institutions. It became utterly clear also that to be the people of God was not a privilege to be enjoyed but a responsibility to be fulfilled. Some prophets began to entertain the vision of a worldwide mission for Israel, in which she would bring the saving knowledge of God to all peoples. Correspondingly, the thought of God himself was deepened. He was understood to be not just the God of Israel but the God of all the earth.

Out of this period of radical rethinking come the servant songs, by the prophet known as Deutero-Isaiah.[12] These songs, perhaps, carry the self-understanding of the first people of God to its uttermost limits. Israel is the servant whom God upholds, and his destiny is 'to bring forth justice to the nations'. But this can be accomplished only at the cost of being 'despised and rejected', of being 'bruised for the iniquities' of mankind. Probably only a few members of the people rose to this vision, but in retrospect we can see it as the fulfilling of the meaning that had belonged to the people from the beginning.

Sometimes there is discussion as to whether the servant of the songs is an individual or a community. Like the similar discussion about Abraham, this one leads us to conclude that the servant must be both individual and community. Christians have seen in the servant a prefiguring of Christ, but also of the church, the new people founded by Christ. But the suffering servant is also the Jewish people, down through the centuries to Auschwitz.

We are not to suppose that Jews and Christians are somehow rival claimants to the position of being the people of God. In any case, we have seen that this is not a privilege, in the com-

monly accepted sense. We are not to suppose either that the new
Christian people of God has superseded or abolished the older
people. Rather, in different ways both Jews and Christians have
responded in faith to the call to become God's people, and in
different ways Jews and Christians have both fulfilled the call
and failed to fulfil it.

At any rate, the people, whether Jewish or Christian, has
edges that are not too sharply defined and its destiny overlaps
the destinies of others. We have seen in the chapter how the
Christian community has affinities with the older community
and can learn from it a better understanding of itself. We must
next extend our view to humanity as a whole, for we have seen
many indications that the people of God stands in solidarity
with the whole human race.

Notes

1. Genesis 12.1-2.
2. Louis Bouyer, *L'Eglise de Dieu*, Paris: Cerf, 1970, p.217.
3. Genesis 12.10-20.
4. Genesis 13.2-13.
5. Genesis 18.16-33.
6. I Peter 2.10.
7. Genesis 22.1-19.
8. Exodus 3.1-15.
9. Cf. Hebrews 11.6.
10. Exodus 12-14.
11. Exodus 19-20.
12. Isaiah 42; 44; 49; 53.

IV

The Humanity of the People

There is an obvious ambiguity in the English word 'people'.
When we use the word with an article, and talk of 'a people' or
'the people', then it refers to some more or less distinguishable
part of mankind, a nation or a race or a community. When we
talk simply of 'people', without any article, our reference is
more general; we mean 'human beings'. Up till now we have
been talking of a particular people – the people of God. But we
have already seen that the people of God has rough edges and
merges into ... just people. Whatever else the people of God
may be, it is in the first instance people, human beings, and it
never ceases to be people. Even if it is constituted by an act of
separation, it remains bound in solidarity with all mankind; and
in its priestly function, it seeks, though not in any imperialist
sense, to identify the whole human race with the people of God.

So we now explore the humanity of the people of God, the
condition which they have in common with all people. Many
of the older theological text-books began with a section on
'natural theology'. The starting-point of this was the knowledge
which all rational persons can have of the world, and on the
basis of this knowledge it was believed that God's existence
could be demonstrated and thus a rational basis laid on which
to build up revealed theology. The traditional forms of natural
theology are not in high repute today,[1] but the task which
natural theology tried to perform remains an important one –
that of showing that Christian beliefs are reasonable and can
find support in common experience. But a contemporary natural
theology differs from the older variety in a number of ways. It
does not claim to demonstrate the truth of theological statements, but seeks to make them intelligible and reasonable; it

does not constitute a preliminary to theology, but is rather an accompaniment, integrated into the whole enterprise; and it is more likely to look for its evidences in human nature than in the world at large.

The present chapter could be considered an exercise in contemporary natural theology. We are asking about people, human nature, in the light of modern philosophy, biology, psychology and all the other ways in which man is studied. Do we find tendencies and indications in human nature generally which suggest that men have to be understood theologically as well as biologically, psychologically and so on? Or do we find in people generally traces at least of those characteristics which have come more fully to light in the people of God, so that we can think of the people of God not as some strange anomaly, some weird group of charlatans or deluded persons. but as indeed pilgrims toward a fuller humanity, toward which also the humanity of all men already obscurely points?

But as soon as we ask about people or human nature, we find ourselves confronted with great difficulties. It is not just that there are many conflicting theories about man. It is rather that there seem to be contradictions in man himself. He lives in the tension of opposites that draw him different ways. Some pessimistic writers have concluded that man is a mistake in the universe, a cancerous offshoot that has got out of control and threatens the whole. On the other hand, one might say that precisely the contradictions and tensions of the human condition are what give hope, for these seem to indicate that humanity is not a finished product but something striving to be born and only to be fully revealed in the future (if it can survive). The very theories that man holds about himself and the ideals of humanity that he fashions can themselves become powerful factors in shaping the reality of mankind.

There is the further complication that although we talk generally about 'man' or 'people' or 'human nature', human beings are not simply examples of a species. There is a personal uniqueness about every human being and it cannot be disregarded. There have been times in human history when powerful forces, political or ecclesiastical, have tried to fit everyone to a uniform pattern. But always at such times someone has arisen to champion the right of the individual to be himself. In the nineteenth century Kierkegaard protested against the type of thinking which makes man a mere abstraction to be incorporated into a system, and proclaimed the concrete category of the individual as the centre of his philosophy. Yet we seem once more to be caught in a contradiction, for if 'mankind' is an abstraction apart from concrete individual human beings, the individual himself is an abstraction apart from the social context. Thus Kierkegaard's philosophy of the person requires to be corrected by Buber's, according to which there can be no 'I' without a 'thou'. Sometimes it looks as if men must for ever oscillate between a collectivism and an individualism, both equally dehumanizing. Yet it is only out of these conflicting tendencies that there could emerge a true community, a state of affairs in which both the social and the individual poles of human nature are fulfilled. The quest for such community is one of the most fundamental characteristics of man, but its goal has proved elusive. One practical test of the claims of the people of God is to ask whether among them we see at least some glimmerings of that genuine fulfilling community for which all people have a deep longing. We have in fact claimed that a new kind of community has emerged among the people of God, cutting across the old social groupings; though we have at the same time acknowledged that the new community is still far from having attained what it has it in it to become, for it is not guaranteed any infallible automatic advance, and does in fact fall into sin.

But let us return to the theme of the conflicts and tensions in man. He has been described as a multi-level being, and obviously at one level he is an animal. He has an assignable place in the animal kingdom. The theory of evolution has demonstrated his descent from pre-human ancestors and his affinities with existing animals. Biochemistry has gone far to unlock the secrets of the living organism and to show that man's mental life is closely bound up with the chemistry of his body. The science of genetics has shown that each of us is, so to speak, programmed in a unique way, and that such basic personal characteristics as intelligence are probably fixed within fairly narrow limits by genetic inheritance. Beyond any question, man's being is firmly anchored in the animal, the material, the physico-chemical levels of being.

Yet it seems equally clear that man rises above the level of animality. Biological description does not exhaust the meaning of the human being, even when such description is carried to the greatest lengths of complexity. There is a plus that remains. Furthermore, it is this plus which is the most interesting and characteristic feature of man and which apparently begins to transform even his biological character. In human beings, for instance, sexuality is no longer only a physiological function but can become the bearer of personal relations. The relation of physical and mental is not onesided but reciprocal.

The plus that makes man more than animal has been variously named. He was traditionally defined as the 'rational animal', where reason is taken as the specific character that marks man off from animal life in general. What, then, is reason? It may be described in various ways, and is clearly inseparable from language. But what is perhaps most distinctive in the use of reason by man is that it allows him to stand outside himself, so to speak, and to reflect on his own situation and his own actions. In this respect, man may be said to transcend himself, and this is an important and basic difference from a merely animal existence. Other thinkers have preferred to speak of the plus in man as 'spirit'. This, too, is a word that has been used in many senses, and some of them are of dubious validity and might well turn out to be misleading forms of language. Perhaps what is fundamental to the idea of spirit is creativity. Man goes out from himself to build up a whole world shaped by his own spirit – a world of art and science, of public institutions and personal relations. In this respect again man is marked off from the animals. His creativity is another form of transcendence. He transcends his world, for he does not simply adapt himself to it, but rather moulds his world in accordance with his own ideals, so far as this is possible. But it is not only his world that he shapes. Man shapes himself. He is no longer only the product of those natural forces which determine the course of evolution. He has himself a say in the shaping of his future. To express this, we may add the word 'existence' to the words 'reason' and 'spirit'. To exist (in the sense of modern philosophies of man) means that he has no fixed, unalterable essence given to him, but goes out to fashion (within limits) his nature. As Sartre has put it, 'If man, as the existentialist sees him, is not definable, it is because to begin with he is nothing. He will not be anything until later, and then he will be what he makes of himself.'[2] Existence, in the sense just explained, is still another form of transcendence in man. This is an active transcendence, a continuous going forth beyond every position that he has reached into new ways of being that he must define.

I have said that the biological account of man is never exhaustive, and we can now see the reason for this. By its very approach, any natural science can deal only with phenomena which can be objectified. Those forms of transcendence we have noted are not objectifiable. They elude the scientific net. Yet they are certainly not illusory, for we know them at first hand in our very act of existing, and these are the characteristics that belong distinctively to our humanity. Also, we are beginning to see the relevance of the idea of a people of God to the human condition in general, and how an analysis of that human condition points one toward some such conception as a people of God. The command to Abraham to go out from his secure dwelling into an undefined future in order to fashion a truly human people, though it was given thousands of years before modern theories of evolution or philosophies of existence, sees man in the same dynamic self-transcending way in which we think of him today. There is still need of a people who for all people will go out from the securities of modern society in quest of a fuller humanity or peoplehood. We might even compare the call to Abraham with the words of Sartre, quoted above. But there is an important difference. Sartre thinks of man as having to make himself entirely out of his own resources; the biblical story brings in God as the one who not only summons man but guides and sustains him in his quest. Obviously we shall have to explore this difference much more fully.

The contrast between man's animality and that other pole of his being embracing reason, spirit, existence, can be expressed in another and more philosophical way by saying that man lives in the tension of finitude and freedom. His finitude consists in the givenness of his existence. The given is that in man which he did not choose and which is in greater or less degree subject to laws which he did not frame. His body, for instance, is subject to natural forces, is limited in its powers, is dependent on a suitable environment, is liable to injury and disease, is destined eventually to deteriorate and die. His mind, too, has its inbuilt limitations. Yet this finite creature has, within the limits of the given, the exercise of freedom. No empirical science, whether biology or psychology or sociology, can take account of freedom, for this is not an objectifiable phenomenon. Freedom cannot be proved, or disproved. In a sense, freedom is a nothing – the abyss out of which one course of action or another will come. Yet freedom is our most precious possession, and we all in fact believe in it. Man becomes more human, more personal, as his freedom or range of options increases. Yet every increase of freedom brings also an increase of responsibility, and freedom is inseparable from anxiety.

Again, we are brought up against the ambiguity of the human situation, if not indeed its sheer self-contradiction. Can this being in whom freedom and finitude are conjoined make any sense, or is he constituted absurdly so that he must be considered an unfortunate anomaly thrown off by the evolutionary process? For must not his givenness be always troubled by his freedom, so that he cannot live with the placid contentment of the animal? While, on the other hand, his freedom must always be frustrated by his givenness, so that whenever he tries to exercise it and to attain a new level of being, he falls back to where he was before? In a famous essay, Camus compared the human condition to that of the mythical Sisyphus, compelled over and over again to roll a heavy rock up a hill, only to see it each time crash to the bottom.[3] Are we to say, then, that man is absurd? Must his capacity for performance finally fall short of the goals which he sets in his freedom? Or is there a hope that even if there are many failures the goal will be achieved? Here we may remember that in the history of the people of God, too, there were many fallings away, yet through them there persisted a hope. That hope, of course, was based on the promises of God, and again we are driven toward the theological problem.

But there is another matter that claims our attention at this point. Whether one regards man as an unhappy error in the universe or as the noblest work of God or as neither of these, there is agreement among all who take a realistic view of human life that there is a massive disorder in it. The theological term for this disorder is 'sin'. Christian theologians have always taught that sin is universal in human life and that man stands in need of a wholeness which he does not at present have. The same view is held in many other religions. And some atheistic philosophers likewise have not hesitated to speak of man's fall or alienation from an authentically human life, so that they too look for a way of salvation. It is true that in modern times there has been a tendency to discount the sinfulness of man, and to believe that his condition steadily improves with the increase of knowledge and its application. But this naïve belief, as Kant remarked, 'has certainly not been deduced from experience – the history of all times cries too loudly against it'.[4] The history of our own time undoubtedly does.

A doctrine of the universality of sin implies that man has not only started off with a difficult constitution to manage, but that he has somehow started off on the wrong foot. There has taken place a distortion which prevents both the fulfilment of the individual and the development of a healthy social order. The experiment of a being in whom are conjoined freedom and finitude must have been from the very beginning fraught with the possibility of disorder. Indeed, as Reinhold Niebuhr has cryptically said, sin, if not necessary, seems to have been at any rate inevitable.[5] For how could man live in the tensions we have described – animality and rationality, individualism and collectivism, finitude and freedom – without falling on the one side or the other? The sins of indulgence and sloth arise from the victory of animality over rationality; the sins of pride from an exaggerated freedom that has forgotten finitude; the sins of acquisitiveness and aggression from an individualism that has forgotten responsibility, and the sins of complacency and conformism from a collectivism that is equally irresponsible. In the past, sin has too often been conceived in individual terms, but there are also corporate sins which have deadly effect, distorted social and political structures which oppress and dehumanize. If there is a remedy for sin, then, it is not a simple one. It cannot be just the conversion of individuals, leaving social structures unchanged; but neither can it be the restructuring of society without a change in the persons who compose it. Something like a miracle is required – a change affecting both the individual and corporate dimensions of life together; in other words, a new *people*, a genuine community. So again we see the relevance of the people of God to the general condition of man-

kind. And this people does claim to be founded on a miracle
which made possible a new life. For a miracle is essentially an
event of grace or revelation, lighting up a situation so that we
see in it possibilities to which we were blind before.

While I have stressed the universality of sin, as any realistic
account of man must do, I do not think that one can accept the
doctrine that man is totally immersed in sin, the doctrine of a
'total depravity'. For if man were totally depraved, he would
not even be conscious of his sinful state or be made uneasy by
it. Only because there persists in the human race something of
an original righteousness, more original than original sin, can
there be awareness of sin and any desire to overcome it. In more
theological language, this original righteousness can be expressed by saying that man was made in the image of God; and
although that image has been marred by sin, it has not been
totally effaced. It speaks of a destiny to which men know themselves obscurely called even in the sinful condition of the race,
and the fact that men go on hopefully striving toward that
destiny is itself a powerful argument against any view, atheistic
or theological, that would write man off as an absurdity or an
incorrigible sinner.

The view of man existing in tensions, deflected by sin and yet
striving for a more authentic life, is one that is well founded, for
it is supported by evidences accessible to all. What it brings
before us is a situation which implies something like the idea of
a people of God for its solution. The implication is twofold –
negative and affirmative. On the negative side, the overwhelming tensions of human life and the apparent inevitability of sin
suggest that man is trapped in a situation from which there is
no exit unless indeed there is the possibility of that opening on
the new which we call grace or revelation and which creates a
people of God, a community living not by itself but by God's
grace, and not for itself but for all people. On the affirmative
side, there is the never-extinguished drive in man toward the
transcendence of any given state and toward the realization of
an obscurely grasped image which is both the image of God
and the image of an authentic humanity. God, as Karl Rahner
has expressed it, is the Whither of the transcendence in man.[6]
The people of God, in this sense, is that community of human
beings who have made this image their ultimate concern and

who are consciously pressing toward the goal which it represents.

To inquire, then, about people in general is to raise the question of an authentic human community and so to be pointed to the idea of a people of God. For the people of God simply seeks to realize the possibility of a true humanity that is in all people. In this chapter, we have approached the problem from the side of people, but we have not been able to avoid language about God. We must now go on to explore further this God-language.

Notes

1. See below, p.36.
2. Jean-Paul Sartre, 'Existentialism is a Humanism', in *Existentialism from Dostoevsky to Sartre*, ed. W. Kaufmann, Cleveland: World Publishing Co., 1956, p.290.
3. Albert Camus, 'The Myth of Sisyphus', in the same collection, pp.312ff.
4. Immanuel Kant, *Religion within the Limits of Reason Alone*, New York: Harper & Row, 1960, p.15.
5. Reinhold Niebuhr, *The Nature and Destiny of Man*, London: Nisbet, 1941, vol. I, p.266.
6. Karl Rahner, *Theological Investigations*, London: Darton Longman & Todd, 1961-8, vol. IV, p.51.

V

God and the People

The expression 'people of God' brings together two terms, 'people' and 'God'. In the last chapter we discussed the meaning of 'people' and found that the discussion pointed us in the direction of the other term, 'God'. What is a people *of God*? We have no difficulty in understanding expressions like 'the people of Athens' or 'the people of Belgium', but 'the people of God' introduces a different kind of language. The word 'God' here indicates a dimension in the life of this community which differentiates it from communities based on kinship or political organization. This is a community of faith, a community that has been grasped and formed by an ultimate concern; and God-language is the language that tries to express this.

But if the people of God is the community whose distinctive character is expressed in the phrase 'of God', then can that community have the pioneering role which we have been ascribing to it as the community charged with leading all people into a fuller humanity? For nowadays a people whose very description involves God-talk will seem to many to be more of a survival from an earlier age than a pioneering community. Has not God-language to a large extent become obsolete and unintelligible? Does God play any significant part in the lives of modern men?

In many ways, it seems that God has no longer anything to do in the world of the scientific and technological age. Men once prayed to God for rain, but now they seek to produce it artificially; they once depended on God for good crops, but they have learned that scientific methods of agriculture are more reliable in producing the desired results; in former times they besought God to stay the plague, but now modern medicine proves itself the most efficient way of combating disease. Even in the moral sphere, God seems no longer needed. Where once a man might have prayed that God would deliver him from an insidious addiction, let us say, he may nowadays turn to some form of therapy; though here it is proper to note that the results are less reliable than in the case of the natural applications of science. Nevertheless, it looks as if the empire in which God once held sway has been greatly reduced, and one could not avoid the question whether his domain might eventually be completely eliminated.

The expression 'the death of God' refers in the first instance to the cultural fact that large areas of human experience once supposed to be controlled by God or the gods are understood today to be determined by quite ungodlike natural happenings within the world, and the more man understands how these events happen, the more he can control them himself. One aspect of the complex process of secularization has been the gradual disentanglement of the natural world from supposed supernatural control, and the corresponding extension of human control so that the natural world has become increasingly a humanized world. To be sure, the extension of human control has not been an unmixed blessing, but it is not something from which we can or should turn back. But as man understands and takes over into his control more and more of what was once left to the caprice of unknown powers, his need for God seems to diminish. Even a century and a half ago, Schleiermacher could write of 'the sense of absolute dependence'[1] as the essence of religion and our surest pointer to the reality of God. But how can the human race have that sense today?

Are we to say that there is a reduced area where God still functions? But what is it? I have pointed out that even the moral life can be brought to some extent within the control of humanly operated techniques. But in any case, we would be assigning to God a precarious and undignified role if we left him presiding over those diminishing segments of life which our science has not yet understood and our techniques have not yet invaded.

Are we, then, to dispense with God altogether and embrace atheism? Even some Christian theologians of modern times, in despair of arriving at any viable conception of God in face of a secularized culture, have recommended a Christian atheism.

But I believe myself that whatever the intellectual difficulties of belief in God, those of atheism are even greater. As philosopher Charles Hartshorne has recently written, 'The properly formulated theistic and religious view of life and reality is the most intelligible, self-consistent and satisfactory one that can be conceived.'[2] But it is very important that we should pay attention to the words 'properly formulated' in Hartshorne's assertion. The theistic view has often been badly formulated, so that the atheistic critique of belief in God has at many points been justifiable. Naïve mythological ideas of God have persisted, although the mythological mentality has on almost every other subject long since been displaced by the scientific mentality. Again, man has projected his own desires and fancies upon God so that God comes to be domesticated, as it were; he is no longer a power confronting man but has been harnessed to human needs and turned into an object of wish-fulfilment. Theology, we have seen, is not a static science, for doctrine requires development.[3] Of all Christian doctrines, the doctrine of God is the one which at present needs to be rethought and developed both in the light of our contemporary knowledge and of the tradition. For it is not only a case of needing to update our conception of God and purge it of antiquated ideas; it is equally important to rescue it from the distortions that keep arising from our own wishful thinking. In other words, we must let God be God, and not what we wish him to be.

Let us at this point recall some of our earlier discussions where, in one way or another, we have touched on the question of God. The people of God, we have seen, was brought into being by experiences described by such words as 'grace' and 'relevation' – experiences which are not planned by those who have them, but seem to come from beyond themselves as a gift which lets them see life in new ways and even confers new life; 'God' is the name used for the source of such experiences. The People makes the response of faith, an ultimate commitment to that which has come to be known in the revelatory experience; that toward which the commitment of faith is directed as an ultimate concern ordering the pattern of the people's life is, once more, 'God'. We have seen, too, that God is named 'I am', the dynamic source of being; he is therefore also the liberating power of history, that which enhances the being of the people; and, paradoxically, he is the inmost demand, for only in obedience to the inward moral demand are men set free to become more fully persons in a more truly human community.

Already in these preliminary hints there is sketched out a basic concept of God. He is the fundamental act of being and from him everything flows; he is active in all things, enhancing their being. The people of God testifies especially to the truth of these statements about God in its own experience. He has brought the people into being, and in its history he is building up the life of the people into a fullness and dignity which reflect in the image of humanity the inexhaustible richness of his own life. Already in the thought of God as conferring and enhancing the existence of finite beings there lies the understanding that God is love; and already in the thought of his many-sided activities at many levels, yet all flowing from a single source, there is a recognition of the diversity-in-unity of God, classically expressed in the Christian doctrine of the Trinity, or, better designated, Triunity.[4]

It is clear that the emerging concept of God described in the last paragraph has nothing to do with a God restricted to what might be called the 'left over areas' of life – the kind of God that we can ignore for most of the time, except when we call him in to explain something that science does not seem able to explain, or to help us in some practical emergency for which no technique seems to avail. On the contrary, the God we have described – and the description was based on testimonies culled from the experience of the people of God – is very much a God at the centre. He is not the answer to a few odd questions that cannot be brought, for the time being at least, within the scope of scientific and technical knowledge. He is rather an answer to the most basic questions of all, questions that underlie all others. What is most real? What is most valuable? What, if anything, deserves our utter allegiance? These questions also make it clear that belief in God (or disbelief) is no purely intellectual matter. One's 'feel' for life and one's scale of priorities must be very different according as one believes that the ultimate reality is the subject of adoration or is not.

I think we can also say that the emerging concept of God – and let us remember again that it is based on the Judaeo-

Christian testimony – has nothing to do with a God of wish-fulfilment. From the day that he commanded Abraham to quit the security of the city for the desert, God has given his people no excuse for settling down in comfort. He is the demanding God, a restless force always leading the people on into the new and unknown. And just as he himself is a God who gives, he calls his people to a costly priestly function. However 'God' may have been perverted in men's minds or replaced with idolatrous fictions, the God to whom the people testify in their history is no gratifier of their wishes.

But let me come back to those basic questions which, it was claimed, underlie all other questions and are the questions to which the word 'God' gives an answer – questions about the real, the valuable and so on. Let us look at some examples in more detail.

Let us suppose that a time came when all the questions of science had been answered. Those are questions about *how* events happen in the world. No science raises the question *why* there is a world at all, rather than a chaos or nothing whatever. Yet this is the most interesting and exciting question of all. Some people would say it is a question that cannot be answered and therefore cannot even be significantly asked. I think that many philosophers nowadays have turned away from this posi-tivist prejudice.[5] But in any case serious-minded people will continue to ask the question, and to some extent all of us assume some kind of answer to it in the practical attitudes which we adopt. To answer the question 'Why a world?' by the word 'God', conceived as the people of God has conceived him, is equivalent to saying that the world exists because of love, and if love is thus the ultimate reality, it must be also the ultimate concern in practice.

Can this be proved? It must frankly be acknowledged that an assertion about the world as a whole cannot be tested in the ways that are possible in the case of scientific hypotheses relat-ing to limited areas of phenomena within the world. But it does not follow that an assertion about the world as a whole is vacuous or completely untestable. We have noted that the old-style natural theology was too ambitious in its claims to prove the existence of God. Yet if anyone asserts this existence and claims that God is love, he must confront his assertion with what we know about the natural world through the sciences. It seems to me that when we do this, there are several considerations which support the theistic interpretation of reality. They certainly fall short of proof, but on such matters we cannot look for more than probability. What we see is, in the first place, a world with structure and order – not a chaos but a reliable universe in which, as Bertrand Russell has expressed it, 'number holds sway above the flux'.[6] But this universe is not just a vast impersonal ordered process, though that would be remarkable enough. It has brought forth persons, and personal life is just as much a part of the universe and a clue to its character as chemical process – indeed, more so, for it is far more complex. And this personal life is not a kind of extra. On the contrary, it would seem that the universe is, so to speak, programmed to give birth to the living and the personal. But water does not rise higher than its source. If the universe is programmed this way, must we not suppose that the creative force at work in it is itself at least living and personal? I repeat, of course, that we are dealing here with probabilities, not certainties. There are many ambiguities in the picture, and above all there is the fact of evil, of which more will be said later.[7] We speak of faith, no knowledge. But it is a reasonable faith which is compatible with the observed facts. Furthermore, both in the believing community and in individual experiences, this faith shows itself capable of throwing light on many aspects of man's life in the world. There is no other interpretation which makes so much sense.

Let us now consider another basic question to which the word 'God' professes to give an answer. When we turn our attention from nature to human life, we may recognize moral obligation as one of our profoundest experiences. Every day we have to ask ourselves in changing situations, 'What ought we to do?' But underlying all the questions about particular situations of obligation is the question, 'Why *ought* I to do anything at all?', or, 'What is oughtness?'. We are so constituted that we know deep within us that we cannot deny the power of obligation without at the same time denying our own status as persons. There is an ultimacy in moral obligation which cannot be exhaustively explained in psychological or sociological terms. No doubt the particular forms of obligation can be shown to depend on social pressures, as Freud has made clear in his conception of the superego. But all such conceptions presuppose a basic obligation to become persons in community, and this basic obligation is not itself an invention of the self or the society. When we refer it to 'God', we are saying it is built into the structure of reality. Moral obligation is another clue to the way things are. A universe which has brought forth moral beings is not itself indifferent to morality. Yet moral obligation is not just 'God's will'; it is more fundamental, for it belongs to the being of God in the sense that it is a basic 'given'. It means that in our world there are some ways that lie open to fuller personal and communal life; and there are other ways that can only diminish and eventually destroy us.

One could go on and describe other possible approaches to God. No one of them, taken by itself, is conclusive, any more than the examples we have considered of the approaches from the natural world and from moral obligation. But perhaps they have a cumulative effect as they all converge on God, understood as an ultimate spiritual reality. We have also to remember that these approaches do not stand on their own, but have to be taken in conjunction with the experiences of grace and revelation on which all communities of faith are founded. I do not think that many people have come to believe in God through pondering such questions as 'Why a world?' or 'What is moral obligation?' These are important questions and have to be taken into account in a reasoned theological analysis of faith, but they are subsequent to faith itself and rarely or never the cause of faith. Faith has its origin in such horizon-expanding events as the life and death of Jesus Christ in Christian experience or the deliverance from Egypt in Jewish experience, and arguments for or against the reality of God come along only later when there takes place reflection on the meaning of the revealing experience. Yet faith and revelation cannot be left standing by themselves. Revelation is not self-authenticating. The intelligent believer must set it in the context of his total experience and ask how far it is supported by that experience.

God, by the very meaning of the expression, is unique. He is, strictly speaking, incomparable. How, then, can we receive a revelation of God or form a concept of him or even utter his name? Our language has been developed for talking about the finite entities we meet within the word – people, trees, hills, automobiles, plays, historical events and all the multitude of components that go to make up a world. But how can we talk of God, who is not another finite being to be added to the list? Perhaps it should be said first that often it is not necessary to say anything at all; before God and concerning God, there will sometimes be a holy, wondering silence. But, as rational beings, we have to use language, and in fact our ordinary language can be 'stretched' in various ways so that it expresses something of what we have learned of God. Our language about God is not a literal, matter-of-fact language, such as we might use about the weather. It is when people have insisted on taking God-language literally that they have made God into another finite being and the whole notion of God becomes incredible. God-language tries to point us beyond the obvious literal meanings of words, and of course the figurative use of language is something that we know in our everyday speech as well.

There are two principal forms of God-language, corresponding to the two ways in which, as we have seen, our human nature itself points to God.[8] Man is pointed to God negatively by his sense of finitude, and this gives rise to the 'way of negation' in speaking of God. Many of the words we use about God are negative words – infinite, immortal and the like. They try to express the notion of a being who is free from the limitations of our finite condition, and they do this by denying that God is limited or given over to death or subject to any other quality which is specifically that of a finite being. This negative speech about God may seem to say very little, but it does mark off the uniqueness of God and guards against the error of reducing him to a manageable factor among others, for then he would not be God at all, but an idol. But as well as the way of negation, we speak of God in the way of analogy. We have seen that on the affirmative side, man is in process of self-transcendence. There is always a 'beyond' into which he is called to advance. Whatever is affirmative in human life – wisdom, goodness, love and so on – points beyond itself, and no matter how far we advance in these qualities, there is never an end in sight. If God is ultimate reality and ultimate value, he must be at the limit of all these affirmative qualities, a limit beyond what we can imagine, yet to which we are pointed when we say 'God is love' or 'God is wise'.

Because our language about God is not literal but evocative, it is often paradoxical. Whatever we say has to be qualified by saying something else to balance it. If we speak of God as 'above' the world, we have also to speak of him as 'within' the world. This is not a contradiction, but arises from the inevitable imprecision of our language. God's relation to the world is unique. If we try to hint at it by using the metaphor of spatial relations, we would give a one-sided and distorted view if we spoke of God *only* as 'above' or *only* as 'within'. We say he is both above and within. Literally, if one were talking about finite objects in world space, this would seem to be nonsense; but analogically it helps to elucidate a unique complex relationship. This relation between God and the world will be further explored in the next chapter.

Notes

1. Friedrich Schleiermacher, *The Christian Faith*, Edinburgh: T. & T. Clark, 1928, p.12.
2. Charles Hartshorne, *Creative Synthesis and Philosophic Method*, London: SCM Press, 1970, p.276.
3. See above, p.2.
4. See below, p.73.
5. See Milton K. Munitz, *The Mystery of Existence*, New York: Appleton-Century-Crofts, 1965.
6. Bertrand Russell, *Autobiography*, London: Allen & Unwin, 1967-9, vol. I, p.13.
7. See below, pp.50f.
8. See above, p.34.

VI

The Environment of the People

In exploring the meaning of the expression 'people of God', we have quite naturally spent most of the time in elucidating the two terms, 'people' and 'God'. But in the course of this exploration, we have found a third term coming in – 'world'. The people does not exist in a vacuum or in a purely spiritual mode of existence. Thus it is not enough for theology to deal only with the relation of the soul to God, though people have sometimes mistakenly supposed that this is what theology is about. The people relates to God in a world and through a world, and theology must give some account of the world and its place in the life of faith.

The world is known in the first instance as environment, the enveloping reality within which we live. In one sense, the environment, as physical reality, is foreign to us. We cannot relate to it as we relate to other people. It stands over against us, silent, impersonal, indifferent. On the other hand, we are bound to it in the most intimate ways and dependent on it at every moment. Our life is sustained by an environment which must be within a certain range of temperature and pressure and which must make available to us a steady supply of oxygen, water and all the other substances needed to support life. We cannot live apart from it. We are indeed ourself part of that tenuous ecological system which has grown up on the surface of the earth, both affecting it and becoming affected by it. Our evolutionary roots lie deep in the physical universe and we remain anchored to it. People without an environment is a mere abstraction of thought. Even in their relations with one another, people need their environment, for they communicate through their bodies and through such physical media as their bodies may use. Likewise our knowledge of God is mediated through worldly realities.

The question of the environment has become a burning issue in the contemporary world. Through science and technology, man has greatly extended his control over the environment. He has shaped it to his needs and has drawn from it substances and energies that have enriched his life in innumerable ways. Yet in this very process of extending his control, he has encountered threatening side effects. As killing diseases are reduced or eliminated, man's own numbers have increased at a staggering rate; through reckless exploitation, some natural resources are becoming depleted; pollution of the air, the rivers, lakes and seas, through industry or the uses of chemicals in agriculture, poses a serious threat to health; the destruction of wild life, apart from any other effects, makes the earth less interesting and less beautiful. One could go on with this perplexing catalogue. What has become clear is that men need a philosophy of nature. The exploitation of the world can be controlled and rightly directed only if there is some overall understanding in the light of which valuations can be made. Western man is the specialist, and it has been because of his ability to isolate limited manageable problems that he has been able to advance so far in his understanding and control of nature. But he seems at the same time to have become less capable of seeing things in their wholeness and interrelatedness (witness his modern distaste for metaphysics), and so his efforts are not coordinated by any clear vision or goal.

The Judaeo-Christian tradition does in fact offer an overall understanding of the world, a kind of basic philosophy of nature, in its doctrine of creation. Such an understanding is, of course, quite different from any scientific understanding of natural phenomena. The doctrine of creation, like other theological doctrines, brings to expression a total attitude. To think of the world as God's creation is not to hold some theory about its origin but to experience it as an environment which one can trust and toward which one can be both free and responsible.

The doctrine of creation has its roots in man himself and especially in his awareness of the finitude and contingency of his existence.[1] He finds himself already in an existence which he did not choose or bring about, and most ancient peoples had their myths of creation, telling how the gods had created their own ancestors. We have seen that the people of God understood itself as called into existence by God and as continuing to live under his grace. This people, too, had its creation stories – the myth of how God made man and set him in the garden of Eden,[2] and the more sophisticated and much later story of how he made the world in successive stages over a period of time.[3] For if man knew his own creaturely status, he could see that the world around him is made up of entities that are finite like himself, and so he must suppose that they, too, owe their existence to God.

In the biblical stories, God *makes* man and all the other creatures. It is no ordinary making, for it is a making out of nothing, and in that respect unique, and radically different from the making done by a craftsman who fashions an already existing material. God gives existence as well as essence. But the analogy of making is inadequate in another way to the unique idea of creation. 'Making' suggests a relation between the maker and what is made that is quite external and impersonal. But God's creating, as a sharing in the gift of existence, must be understood as a much more intimate kind of relation. If we think of the relation of an artist to his work, we have a better analogy. The artist certainly brings the work into being, but while it is not literally a part of himself, he has in a true sense put himself into it. It is not merely external to him. At this stage we may recall the earlier point that God is both above and within the world.[4] This now gets its further meaning in relation to creation. As creative source, God is prior to the world and transcendent of it; yet because he loves the world and it is his own work, in a sense of which the human work of art affords some distant analogy, God is also immanent in the world. It is very important that both aspects of God's relation to the world should be made clear in any statement of the doctrine of creation.

The practical bearing of these remarks becomes obvious when we look again at the question of man's relation to the world and his exploitation of nature. It may be fairly claimed that a balanced doctrine of creation provides the best foundation on which to develop a good relation between man and his environment. On the one hand, when the world is seen as creation, we understand that it belongs to the finite order. The world is not divine. Primitive peoples thought of every natural phenomenon as a direct manifestation of the divine. Every stream and mountain and tree was the abode of a spirit. But gradually nature was cleared of these imaginary divinities, until it came to be understood as we understand it today in terms of modern science. It is generally agreed that the biblical doctrine of creation had an important part in the rise of the scientific attitude, for by teaching that the world is God's work and therefore not itself divine, it encouraged man to explore the world and to turn it to his use. Sometimes people are alarmed as man increases his power and knowledge, and seems to become almost godlike himself. But if the doctrine of creation is true, man is fulfilling his destiny in the expansion of his knowledge and power. He is not setting himself up as a rival to God but carrying out the task which he finds assigned to him in the created order. Through his science and technology, he is able to make his life in the world first more tolerable and then more human. A bishop in the poverty-stricken, underdeveloped north-east of Brazil writes: 'The more boldly man advances, the more his deeds will be a hymn to the glory of the Father Creator.'[5] But these remarks remain one-sided until we have filled in the rest of the picture. It has been a one-sided preoccupation with the mastering of nature that has led to the grievous waste and destruction of the environment in industrial countries and to the development of a consumer mentality which in turn aggravates the acquisitive and aggressive tendencies in man. It is a balanced, not a one-sided, doctrine of creation that can save us from such consequences. For we have seen that God is not only the transcendent maker, he is also the immanent spirit who puts himself into his works. Man has therefore a responsibility in the face of creation which may not be recklessly exploited. Indeed, we still know so little of the universe that it would be rashly presumptuous for us in our tiny corner to suppose that man's dominion is to extend everywhere.

The two sides of the doctrine of creation may be expressed from the point of view of man. He is himself a creature, part of the created universe and dependent for his being on God. Yet his is a 'middle state'. For he has a share in creativity. As we have seen, the expression 'absolute dependence' is not entirely appropriate.[6] Man is the unique (as far as this earth is concerned) creature who is also co-creator or, better expressed, co-worker with God in shaping a creation which is still on its way. Man's position in relation to the rest of creation is therefore not that of absolute disposer, but that of steward or guardian or even (to recall one of the functions of the people of God) priest.

The very existence of a world in which there are free but finite creative beings is itself a remarkable evidence for the reality of a God of love. For it must have been love that led the ultimate creative source, God, to share with finite creatures not only existence but even a measure of participation in his own creativity. Belief that God is love must also raise the question whether the world ever had a beginning. For if God is at heart outgoing and self-giving love, must we not suppose that he has always been creating and sharing his being? We must again remind ourselves that the doctrine of creation does not claim that there was a time when God was on his own before there was a world. It would be very difficult to conceive of any time before the world, since time itself can only be experienced or measured by events which happen within the world. It may well be the case that the present universe had an origin, but this is a question for science, not theology. The Christian doctrine is content to claim that the world of finite beings, including man, points beyond itself to a creative sustaining power, the God of love.

We must dwell a little longer on the question of God's relation to the world. On the interpretation of creation given here, this relation cannot be an entirely one-sided or asymmetrical one, as in the traditional monarchical model of God. On that model, God was conceived as an absolute ruler, above the world and controlling it, but not affected by it. Creation itself was sometimes conceived as an arbitrary act on God's part, as if it would make not the slightest difference to him whether he had a creation or not. But if we take seriously the doctrine that God is outgoing love, then it must lie in his very nature to create. Creation is no arbitrary act on his part, though we need not say that it is a necessary act either. It simply flows from his being as love. But if this is so, the monarchical model of God's relation to the world is most inadequate. We must conceive the relation rather as an organic one, in which God is affected by the world as well as affecting it. One cannot love without becoming vulnerable to the object of one's love. In creation God, we may say, takes a risk. This is especially the case when his universe brings forth personal beings who are themselves finite centres of freedom and creativity. There is the risk that they will turn against God. Thus in creating God also limits his own power.

Here we may recall two traditional words that have been used about God and that seem to call for some explanation in view of what has just been said – 'immutable' and 'omnipotent'. God's immutability has sometimes been taken to mean that, like some impassive despot, he remains utterly unmoved and unchanging even if the world goes to wrack and ruin. Christians have rightly felt that there is something wrong with that image of God. And the reason for their uneasiness, as I have said, is that if God is love, then he exposes himself to the vulnerability of love and cannot be immutable in the sense of being utterly unaffected by events in his creation. God's immutability does not mean that he exists in a state of frozen immobility (that would be the death of God!), but that there is a faithfulness and unchanging love in all his ceaseless activity. God's omnipotence, again, has been taken to mean that he can do anything. But if he is a God of love and not a capricious monarch, then he cannot act against his own nature. What he does cannot go counter to love or wisdom or truth, and it will not wipe out the freedom he has conferred on his creation. 'God is omnipotent,' wrote Augustine: 'He cannot die, he cannot be deceived, he cannot lie ... How many things he cannot do! Yet he is omnipotent!'[7] God's omnipotence means that he is the source of all being and all energy, 'creation's secret force'; and since this is an ordered being and energy, God's omnipotence could never be taken in the arbitrary sense of ability 'to do anything'. Perhaps the word 'omnipotent' (like the word 'immutable') is unfortunately chosen and can be misleading. But theological terms, like those of other sciences, have to be learned and used in the context of the discourse to which they belong. No one would suppose, for instance, that if a biologist describes an animal as omnivorous, it can eat concrete.

The doctrine that the world is the creation of a God of love has always faced one major difficulty – the fact of evil. If religious beliefs are not to be merely escapist, they must be confronted with the facts of experience; and evil in its various forms seems to be a constant and unavoidable element in all human experience. This fact of evil is a standing challenge to belief in God and certainly contradicts any facile belief that God orders everything for our convenience, and any easy-going optimism based on such a belief. The creation story tells us: 'God saw everything that he had made, and behold, it was very good', but things keep happening in our daily experience which put this affirmation in question.

Various solutions can be offered to the problem of evil. None of them are conclusive, but they have some cumulative effect. It can be said that human life is possible only in a regularly ordered reliable universe, and that it is inevitable that such regular workings must sometimes conflict with particular interests. Again, it can be said that persons can come into being only through struggle and the overcoming of resistance, so that God could not have brought finite persons into being in a universe where everything was already perfected, but only in a universe still in process of creation where these finite persons might themselves join in the toil of building toward its perfection. Further, we do not know to what extent the disorder or sin of man's own existence – a necessary risk, as we have seen, in creation – has infected his environment, for long before there was any talk of an ecological crisis, theologians had speculated that man's fall into sin must have had its results in a cosmic fall, a disordering or pollution, as it were, of the total environment.

On the dynamic view of creation presented in this chapter, its goodness is in any case still coming to be. The creation was not a finished product made at a given time in the past, but a continuing process in which man now has a responsible part to play. The fact that man lives on in hope is itself a testimony to a deep conviction that the world is essentially good and this goodness can be more and more fully manifested. If easy-going optimism is an error, so is pessimism. Men do in fact choose life rather than death, for they believe that on balance life is good, and it can become better.

Since we understand creation not as an event of the remote past but as the continuing relation between God and his world, we cannot make a sharp distinction between creation and providence. But when we use the word 'providence', we are call-

ing attention to God's unceasing care for his world and his
involvement in it. Providence is not a fate which fixes everything in advance of its happening – this would contradict the
very idea of a creation which has brought forth as its finest
flower beings who are able to exercise freedom and a limited
measure of independence. Neither does providence mean that
God keeps interfering in the world's affairs to prevent things
going wrong – this would contradict the idea of a world in which
there is order and reliability. But to believe in providence does
mean to accept that history is shaped not only by men and
nature but by God. Our earlier discussions of the history of the
people of God have shown how he acts – by calling, constraining, challenging, demanding; by acts of grace and revelation
mediated through his creatures; by preserving and re-establish-
ing the people in times of falling away. These are not 'dramatic'
acts. They mesh with the ordinary course of events. But to the
eye of faith they are miracles; that is to say, they are seen in
their full depth and significance as flowing from the God of love
who is communicating himself in and to his creation. We
have still to consider the greatest of all such events – how God
in a new way came into his creation in the person of Jesus Christ.

But before we leave the theme of creation, there is another
matter on which I shall briefly touch. Our discussion has been
mainly concerned with nature, those levels of being which
stand below man in the evolutionary scale. Both Christian and
Jewish theology, however, has traditionally had a doctrine of
angels – intelligent spiritual beings who excel man in their
capacities. They are usually represented as good, though we
must not forget that the tradition speaks also of fallen angels.
No doubt much of the lore concerning angels is poetry and
mythology. Yet there is an important theological truth in this
doctrine. It teaches that man is not the measure of all things.
Indeed, now that we know how vast and unimaginable is the
extent of the universe in space and time, and that this universe
seems to be programmed, as it were, to bring forth first living
creatures and then persons, it becomes statistically highly prob-
able that there do exist and will exist many races of spiritual
beings capable of becoming, as we are, peoples of God. Recognition of this reinforces our understanding of our role in the
universe – not to be masters, having everything at our absolute

disposal, but to be stewards and guardians, co-workers with God and his other creatures in a creative venture that reaches beyond what we can imagine.

Notes

1. See above, p.31.
2. Genesis 2.4-25.
3. Genesis 1.1-2.3.
4. See above, p.44.
5. Dom Helder Camara, *Revolution through Peace*, New York: Harper & Row, 1971, p.22.
6. See above, p.47.
7. Augustine, *De Symbolo: Sermo ad Catechumenos*, 2.

VII

Christ the Focus of the People

We have now explored in a general way the primary theological datum, the people of God. We have seen something of the basic significance of this people, of its function and responsibility, of its ties with the whole human race, of the meaning of its faith in God, of its relation to the environing world. Now within the context of what has been brought to light in these explorations, we must seek a new clarity and definiteness by turning our attention directly to Jesus Christ, the focal creative reality at the people's heart. He is the founder of that new people of God whose sudden and massive rise transformed the ancient world.[1] At the same time, he is the fulfilment of that first people of God that began with Abraham, and indeed the fulfilment of the obscure aspirations toward a fuller humanity, aspirations as wide as humanity itself. The first interpretative title given to Jesus of Nazareth was Messiah,[2] and this represented him as the fulfilment of the hopes of the first people of God. Yet it was soon understood by the Christian community that the reality which had come to expression in Jesus Christ was not only the fulfilment of messianic expectations, but must have inspired these expectations in the beginning. So we find that Christ is named not only Messiah but the eternal Word,[3] the very meaning and goal of the cosmos already present in the beginning. He is represented as saying of himself: 'Before Abraham was, I am!'[4] Christ is both the founder and the fulfiller, the beginning and the end, the agent of creation and the prototype of creation.

How can such tremendous claims be made for anyone? It sounds like madness. Yet if there is any validity at all to that sense of a constraining power which men call 'God' and which summoned Abraham from his home and worked on all those who came after, the lines converge unmistakably on Jesus Christ as the supreme manifestation of God, the God-man, the incarnate Word.

Christology is that branch of theology concerned with interpreting the significance of Jesus Christ for faith, and it has assumed many forms during the centuries of Christian history. We have seen that the first move was to interpret Jesus as Messiah, and so to connect him with all the beliefs and hopes of the Jewish people. As Christianity moved out into the Greco-Roman world, new ways of interpreting the meaning of Christ had to be found. How would one go about the task of interpretation today, in the secularized societies of the late twentieth century?

We begin with the simple assertion that Jesus was a man, a real human being of flesh and blood and spirit like ourselves. He lived at a particular time, under the emperors Augustus and Tiberius, and in a particular region, the province of Palestine. The real human, historical existence of Jesus is something that nowadays no reputable scholar would deny. We have the testimony of the New Testament writings, supplemented by brief allusions in a few non-Christian writers, notably Tacitus and Suetonius. But the main evidence is simply the indubitable fact of the church itself, the Christian people of God. 'The principal argument the historians have for the existence of Jesus,' writes John Knox, 'is the church's prior knowledge of it, that is, a memory of Jesus which can be traced back continuously through the centuries to the time when the church first emerged into consciousness of itself.'[5]

But our knowledge of Jesus is not confined to the bare fact that he existed, for, in isolation, this would not be very important. We have also a fairly detailed and reliable knowledge of his teaching. The first point to be made about this teaching is that it shared the eschatological expectations of the Jewish people of that time. The existing world-order, so it was believed, would shortly come to an end and be replaced by a new age. It seems likely that Jesus believed that his disciples would see this happen,[6] but in any case his own preaching and deeds were taken to be signs of the inbreaking of the new age. That new age is called in Jesus' teaching the 'kingdom of God'. It forms the subject of many of his parables and is the ever-present background to all his teaching. The coming of the kingdom would mean the judgment of the existing order, the overthrow of all evil and demonic powers, and a new order in which God's perfect reign would be manifested. Inseparable from the eschatological teaching, and dependent on it, is Jesus' ethical teaching. It derives its seriousness and radical character from the expectation of the approaching end of the age. In this end time, which has already begun, men must decide for obedience to God if they would hope to participate in the kingdom. Jesus' ethical teaching is developed in dialectic with the traditional Jewish law, and he carries the demand of God to new lengths of inwardness and radicalness. Contrasting his own teaching with the traditional teaching in a series of antitheses,[7] Jesus teaches that outward conformity to the law is not enough. There must be also inward conformity to God at the very springs of action – in other words, there must be a remaking of humanity. Likewise he criticizes the cultic and ritual demands of the traditional law, such as sabbath observance, and makes the moral demand utterly supreme. This is the demand of love, and it is a love not confined by considerations of kinship or friendship, but love to the 'neighbour', the person who happens to be alongside at any given moment and to whom there is an opportunity of giving help.[8] Another aspect of this radical ethical teaching is Jesus' abandonment of the principle of retribution and his advocacy of non-violence and non-resistance.[9] To the eschatological and ethical aspects of his teaching, there must be added the theological teaching, above all, the understanding of God as Father. This is the same God who has been known in the tradition, but that traditional knowledge is of no avail unless God is now known in the present demand and as the power of the coming kingdom.

Scholars have pointed to many parallels between the teaching of Jesus and that of other Jewish religious teachers. Yet, taken as a whole, Jesus' teaching has a uniqueness that makes it stand out from that of all his contemporaries and predecessors among the Jewish rabbis. It is in many ways so radical that even today theologians debate whether its demands can be taken seriously. In addition, it is given with such authority (as, for instance, in those passages where Jesus presents his own teaching in deliberate contrast with the tradition) that Jesus is immediately distinguished from the common run of teachers.[10]

So far, we have asked about the existence of Jesus and about his teaching, and on both of these matters we have seen that we can have a reasonably well assured knowledge. But what about his life? Can we know about his career, and the kind of person he was? At this point, we come up against greater problems than we have met in dealing with the questions about the existence and teaching of Jesus. The Gospels are not biographies, if by that is meant straightforward chronological accounts of the life of Jesus, the development of his character and thought, and so on. The Gospels are themselves products of the people of God, a people that had been already seized by the gracious and revelatory power of Christ and had made an act of faith in him. Thus their accounts of him are not neutral descriptions such as one might demand from modern 'scientific' historians but presentations deeply infused with the confession: 'We have beheld his glory, glory as of the only Son from the Father!'[11] Although this quotation comes from the Fourth Gospel, in some measure it typifies them all. They are not concerned to relate the 'bare facts' of Jesus' life but to draw attention to his 'glory', to his deeper significance as the bringer of grace and revelation from the Father. Thus the Gospels constitute a peculiar type of literature. Their story is told, as it were, on two levels. On the one hand, they recount words and deeds that were publicly observable. But these observable events are set in the context of an interpretative apparatus – voices from heaven (at the baptism and transfiguration), angelic appearances (at the birth and resurrection), theological explanations (at the passion), references to Old Testament prophecies, and so on.

No doubt many of the events narrated in the Gospels have some factual basis, and nineteenth-century scholars tried hard to disentangle the 'simple facts' from the interpretative apparatus. But it is now generally agreed that their quest for the 'historical Jesus' was an impossible one. The facts have become too firmly fused with the interpretative apparatus to be separable.

This does not mean, however, that we are denied all knowledge of the events of Christ's life and the kind of person he was. Some events force themselves on us as obviously true, especially those that were somewhat embarrassing to the disciples and which they might readily have forgotten or suppressed were they not well known. A good example is Jesus' baptism at the hands of John the Baptist. This was an awkward but undeniable fact, and Matthew in his Gospel tries to find an acceptable explanation for it.[12] Well attested, too, is the crucifixion and the cry of dereliction from the cross,[13] another item which has proved awkward for exegetes. Some other matters, too, are well established – that Jesus performed healings and exorcisms, that he consorted with persons who were outside the social and religious pale, that he was a critic of the religious establishment and came into conflict with it. We can also make some deductions from Jesus' teaching to the kind of life that he lived. The idea sometimes put forward that Jesus was a violent revolutionary, for instance, is flatly contradicted by his teaching on non-violence and the persistence of this teaching among his followers. The overwhelming testimony of the church and the New Testament is to the effect that Jesus' teaching found its supreme exemplification in his own life, and there is no reason to doubt this. On the contrary, if there had been any marked discrepancy between his teaching and his life, it is hard to see how the new people of God could ever have come into being.

However, as I have said, the facts are so firmly fused with the theological and sometimes mythological interpretations of the evangelists that for the most part they can no longer be fully sorted out. There would be no great advantage in sorting them out in any case. To be sure, it is important to establish the general trustworthiness of the Gospels, and I have indicated that this can be done. But beyond that, we are interested not in accumulating 'bare facts' but in exploring the theological significance of Jesus Christ, his meaning for faith; and it is precisely this significance and meaning that the Gospels intend to convey in their mode of presentation.

We shall now consider some climactic moments in the career of Jesus as this is presented in the Gospels. For each of these moments there is a factual, historical event, sometimes more, sometimes less clearly discernible. But in each case that event has been incorporated into an interpretative context designed to bring out its significance for faith.

We begin with the birth. Only the Gospels of Matthew and Luke tell of this event, and their stories are different. However well loved the Christmas stories are, they cannot be deemed to have any more than a minimal factual content. These stories have their rightful and abiding place in liturgy and devotion, but they are poetic rather than historical descriptions. Their whole intention is not to give factual information about the birth of Christ but to assert his significance for the world into which he was born. On the factual side, we can hardly say more than that Jesus must have been born somewhere in Palestine around the end of the reign of Herod the Great. But the whole point of the birth stories is the theological one, contained in the idea of a virginal conception 'by the Holy Ghost of the Virgin Mary'. This is the interpretative element which, retrospectively, seeks to draw out the significance of a birth which, at the time it occurred, must have been an utterly obscure event. The point of the interpretation is that with the coming of Jesus, a new humanity came into existence; a new people, indeed, a new world had been born, because God, in a new way, had come into his creation. And of this new people, called into being by God through Christ, the Fourth Gospel can say that they 'were born not of blood nor of the will of the flesh nor of the will of man, but of God'.[14] The doctrine of the virginal conception of Jesus must not be interpreted in any way that would diminish his true humanity – that would be to undermine the whole idea of incarnation. What the doctrine asserts is that Jesus is a man, born of a woman and in solidarity with all men, yet a man in whom humanity has been raised to a new level, so that the community he gathered about him to share in the new humanity had to confess that this man was from God in a unique and unprecedented manner.

Jesus emerges into public history with his baptism at the hands of John, and we have noted that this is one of the best-attested events of his life.[15] But again the Gospels, looking back and seeing the event in the light of subsequent developments, place upon it a theological interpretation. It is represented as the moment of Jesus' self-consecration to his messianic mission. It may originally have been no more than Jesus' response to the preaching of John and his joining himself to the followers of the Baptist. If we take the humanity of Jesus in earnest, then we must suppose that for him as for other men, his sense of vocation would take time to develop. The writers of the Gospels, looking back from a time when they knew the sequel, tended to foreshorten the perspective of events, and this in turn makes it less easy for us to appreciate the true humanity of Christ, and we get the impression that he only seemed to be a man but had really supernatural insight into the future. But again we have to resist any interpretation that diminishes the humanity of Jesus, for in the long run this diminishes his total significance and leaves us with an unreal mythological figure. It is most unlikely that at the moment of baptism Jesus understood himself to be the Messiah, but what cannot be doubted is that in his early adult life he felt and responded to the prophetic vocation, through the human agency of John. The full shape of that vocation had still to unfold itself. We must not think of Jesus following out a script that had been written in advance, but as meeting a future in which he could see only a certain way ahead at any given time. Yet when he responded to his vocation, he already knew that Jerusalem had a long record of killing the prophets,[16] and it was not long until that tradition of prophetic suffering was exemplified anew in the death of John the Baptist at the hands of Herod Antipas.

The incident of the transfiguration must be accounted almost wholly symbolic. Yet clearly it points to a moment that must have occurred – the moment when the disciples saw Jesus in a new light and perceived his 'glory'. Just as there was development in Jesus' own understanding of his vocation, so there was development in the disciples' understanding and estimate of him. They began by joining themselves to a teacher and prophet, of whom there had been many in Israel. But as they came to know him in depth, he was transfigured before them and they perceived him as the Holy One of God: 'This is my beloved Son!'[17] Whether this happened during the ministry of Jesus, as the Gospels indicate, or only after the resurrection appearances, as some modern scholars argue, is of little importance. The point is that somewhere along the line came this moment of recognition. This incident, like the others, points us to the paradox of Jesus as understood by his disciples and presented in the Gospels – the paradox of a wholly human reality which is at the same time capable of being seen by the eye of faith in a 'depth' or 'glory' that constitutes it a divine revelation.

Most important of all the events in the life of Christ was its end – his sufferings and death. All the Gospels devote much of their space to a detailed account of his last days and hours. The passion narratives have the same twofold reference as the other stories we have considered. There is on the one hand an historical fact, in this case a publicly observable crucifixion. As we have noted, this fact is well attested as fact. It firmly anchors Jesus Christ in the stream of world-history. He 'suffered under Pontius Pilate'. Furthermore, this fact of the crucifixion asserts once again the full humanity of Jesus – he died as all men do, so he was no mythical demigod or angelic revealer, but a mortal man. On the other hand, the passion narratives invest this simple fact of a man's death on a cross with the greatest theological significance, as Christ's atoning work which overcomes sin and liberates the world for a new mode of existence. The cross becomes the symbol of the very essence of Christianity. The 'glory' of Christ is seen above all in his humiliation and death. How can this be so?

In attempting to understand this, we must be careful not to separate Christ's death from the total context of his life. Too often his death has been isolated as his atoning or reconciling work, yet it has its significance when it is seen as the climax and perfecting of everything that had gone before. Indeed, when we consider the death of Jesus, perhaps the first thought to impress us is the amazing congruence of his death with everything that we know about his life and teaching. In ordinary human experience, death comes as an interruption, a blow from outside, a contingency. But it is not so with the death of Christ. It has there an affirmative quality, an action which he takes upon himself to perform rather than a fate which he suffers. It is the action which gathers up all his other deeds in one final and absolute deed of self-giving. It is likewise the action in which he carries to the uttermost limit his obedience to his vocation. Death itself is transformed in this death, for it has become an act of absolute self-giving love. And for this reason, as I have said, it is precisely in Christ's death and humiliation that faith perceives the full measure of his 'glory' – the glory of a new humanity that has transcended to the level of the God-man, in whom God and man are wholly and perfectly at one.

Many analogies have been used to elucidate the meaning of Christ's death. In the early centuries, his passion was depicted

as a battle against the forces of evil and his death on the cross
as a victory over these forces; and, paradoxically, it was so, for
his death, as the church has remembered it, was the triumph
of the affirmative power of love over the destructive powers of
violence and hatred. The notion of sacrifice, familiar in the
religions of the ancient world, has also been widely used as an
interpretative model. We were already introduced to this notion
in considering the projected sacrifice of Isaac in the history of
the first people of God.[18] Now in the death of Christ we may say
that the priestly role of the people of God has been brought to
its highest pitch in Christ's costly atoning work. Less satisfactory is the analogy which thinks of Christ enduring on
behalf of mankind the punishment due to sin. Yet this analogy
has been very influential in the history of Christian thought, and
it certainly does stress the reality of sin in human life, a reality
so enormous that it led to Christ's rejection and his suffering.
No one of these models is by itself adequate, nor is any of the
other models which have been used.[19] But among them they
help to light up the significance of Christ's death as the decisive
breakthrough in history of love and everything that is affirmative.

The death of Jesus is an impressive and significant event, but
according to the testimony of the Gospels, it was not the end of
the story. They go on to tell of the resurrection of Christ. This
last event in the series of climactic moments in the career of
Jesus differs from the preceding ones because it is much more
difficult to say what the historical fact was. Some scholars have
tried to locate the fact in the community, and virtually identify
the risen Christ with the church, the new people of God that
arose after his death and continued his work. Others have
asserted that Christ rose in the kerygma or proclamation of the
church. But theories which reduce the meaning of the resurrection to the dimensions of an event which occurred only in
the community surely do less than justice to the facts. For it
does seem quite certain that there never would have been any
rise of the people of God if that people had not been convinced
that Jesus was risen. Their conviction was founded in the first
instance on the appearances of the risen Christ to some of the
disciples, though later stories were also told about Christ's tomb
having been found empty. What, then, was the nature of those

appearances, on which belief in the resurrection was based and on which therefore the rise of the Christian church depended? Are we to say that they were merely subjective visions – to put it bluntly, hallucinations – in the minds of Mary Magdalene, Peter and the rest? This would be a difficult thesis to maintain, for it seems that after the crucifixion the disciples were in despair and there was no disposition to expect that Jesus would appear to them. Furthermore, one would have to say that the Christian church had been founded on an illusion, and while indeed some people have maintained that this is so, it is hard to believe that a community founded on hallucination could have survived for long, let alone have shown the unparalleled creative and expansive power of the Christian people of God. The history of that people is itself a testimony to the working in it of a living spiritual power. Man is so constituted that he never completes himself in his earthly existence and he hopes beyond death. This is something like a natural pointer to the possibility of resurrection. Would we not expect that if, as we have seen reason to believe, Jesus Christ brought humanity to a new level and even transformed death into something affirmative, then the meaning of resurrection would be made evident in him? And is it also not true that not only those first disciples who reported the 'appearances' but all subsequent generations of Christians have testified to Christ's living presence in the midst of his people, and this present experience is the strongest evidence of the truth of his resurrection?

Let us agree that the resurrection 'in itself' is an event for which we have no parallels and about which we can therefore say very little. The Gospels, too, say nothing about the event in itself, but only about its consequences among the disciples. Yet these consequences are indubitable, and they seem to postulate a prior event, however mysterious, which made them possible. As the one who opens up a new humanity, Christ also opens up the eternal destiny of man.

In this interpretation of the meaning of Jesus Christ, we have begun from the fact of his full humanity. But as we have explored that humanity, we have found in it a depth or a glory beyond the ordinary levels of humanity that we know in ourselves or in other people. That depth cannot be simply defined. It arises out of a unique constellation of factors in Christ – his

self-giving love, his obedience to God's calling, his liberating
and creative relations with others, the authority and perceptive-
ness of his teaching, and so on. As mentioned above, it was
only in course of time that the disciples saw into this unique
depth, and for them the resurrection was the clinching experience. The first preaching was that the man, Jesus of Nazareth,
had been made by God both Lord and Christ.[20] But further
reflection led on to a full doctrine of incarnation. Christ was
seen as the fulfilment of God's purpose from the beginning, he
is the eternal Word of God made flesh.[21] In the words of Hans
Urs von Balthasar, 'The raising of a man to the unique, the only-
begotten, calls for the yet deeper descent of God himself, his
humbling, *kenosis*.'[22]

It has been our intention to make the concept of the people
of God the central and articulating idea in this exposition of
Christian theology. Have we abandoned this intention in dwelling on Jesus Christ as the centre of the whole theological structure? By no means. Jesus Christ has his own uniqueness, but he
is no private individual. Through Mary his mother on the one
hand and through the community which he gathered about
him on the other, he is himself in solidarity with the Christian
people of God, with the first people of God, and with all mankind. He would indeed be unintelligible apart from the community of which we have designated him the 'focus'. The
moments of his life – election, transfiguration, sacrifice, resurrection – concentrate and show in a new clarity and depth,
either by fulfilment or anticipation, the moments of the life of
the community itself.

Notes

1. See above, p.9.
2. Mark 8.29.
3. John 1.14.
4. John 8.58.
5. John Knox, *The Church and the Reality of Christ*, London: Collins, 1963, p.61.
6. Luke 9.27.
7. Matthew 5.21-48.
8. Luke 10.29-37.
9. Matthew 5.38-42.
10. Mark 1.22.
11. John 1.14.
12. Matthew 3.14-15.
13. Mark 15.34.
14. John 1.13.
15. See above, p.58.

16. Matthew 23.37.
17. Mark 9.7.
18. See above, pp.21f.
19. Cf. F. W. Dillistone, *The Christian Understanding of Atonement*, Welwyn: Nisbet, 1968.
20. Acts 2.36.
21. John 1.14.
22. Hans Urs von Balthasar, *A Theology of History*, London: Sheed & Ward, 1963, p.11.

VIII

The People's Life in the Spirit

Still another story is told of Jesus Christ, that of his ascension into heaven. The story presupposes the mythological conception of the cosmos in which heaven is a divine abode beyond the sky. With this mythological imagery there is being expressed the conviction that Christ has moved on to a new mode of existence. We might say that the universal significance and influence of his being has been liberated from the limitations of his particularized existence in space and time. Yet this does not mean that some timeless truths or generalizations have been extracted from the historical existence of Jesus. It means rather that the living and vivifying presence of Christ is henceforth available in all times and all places.

'Why do you stand gazing into heaven?'[1] is the appropriate question addressed to the disciples once Jesus has disappeared from their sight. The question is appropriate because these disciples stand not at an end but at a beginning. Their business is not to try to recall in nostalgic longing the Jesus whom they had known for a little time in their corner of the world, an historical figure who would more and more recede into the past, but to respond to the living spirit of Christ and to extend far beyond that period and region in which the incarnate Word had appeared the new humanity of which he was the centre. The band of disciples was now the body of Christ, his continuing incarnation, the growing edge of the new humanity. And so faithfully did they respond to the living and ascended Christ that, as we have seen, the ancient world was astonished by the massive and sudden rise of a new people of God, the Christian church.[2]

That after the death of their leader a small group of obscure

men, none of them powerful, wealthy or educated, should become
the core of a rapidly expanding and world-transforming move-
ment is itself a fact demanding some explanation. And first we
should listen to the explanation offered by those people themselves. They spoke of being filled with the Holy Spirit, as a
source of inward strength in their lives. Admittedly, their
language was variable and not too clear. They could speak of
the risen Christ, of the spirit of Jesus, of the Holy Spirit, and
these are not always clearly distinguished from each other. But
certainly they were testifying to their experience of a new inward source of power which, they believed, proceeded from God
through Christ. And this testimony cannot be lightly set aside
or given a merely psychological explanation when one pays
attention to the scarcely credible rise of the new community
of the Spirit.

The explosive release of spiritual energy is well depicted in
the familiar story of the events on the Feast of Pentecost. The
disciples were gathered together when of a sudden they were
filled with the Holy Spirit. Apparently they 'spoke with tongues',
that is to say, they engaged in the ecstatic utterances that are
sometimes observed in states of intense spiritual excitement.
But if they spoke with tongues, they also spoke in plain intelligible language. Peter proclaimed the crucified and risen Christ
with such effect that he is said to have made three thousand
converts on that single day.[3]

Possession of or by the Holy Spirit soon came to be regarded
as the mark of the authentic Christian, and the new people of
God came to understand itself as the community of the Spirit.
What then are we to understand by this doctrine of a Holy
Spirit?

The word 'spirit' originally meant 'breath', and its etymology
suggests both the elusiveness of spirit when we try to form a
clear idea of it, and its dynamic character, for the breath is that
which makes alive. The word 'spirit' has already been introduced in an earlier chapter,[4] where it was used to stand for that
capacity in man to go out from himself and to become creative
in the world. When we speak of the 'Spirit' of God, then, we
think of him by analogy with what we know of spirit in human
experience. We have seen that God is not adequately conceived
in terms of transcendence alone, but that in a real sense he puts

himself into his creation.[5] The Holy Spirit is that mode of the divine Being whereby God comes into his creation, not just in passive indwelling but as a creative force. This is God in his nearness to his creatures, and especially to those of his creatures to whom he has given a share of spirit and who stand therefore in a mysterious affinity to himself.

Although the story of the Feast of Pentecost tells of a great new outpouring of the divine Spirit, he had of course always been in the world, as the Old Testament clearly testifies. In the creation narrative, the Spirit is represented as the wind of God blowing over the waters of chaos from which an ordered world arises through the divine creative energy.[6] As the history of Israel unfolds, the Spirit of God is understood as God's action in history, especially through exceptional individuals, heroes and prophets, who are said to have had the Spirit. But there is also the vision of the descent of the Spirit on the whole people, to bring them new life.[7]

In the New Testament, the Holy Spirit is associated in the first instance with Jesus Christ. He was 'conceived by the Holy Spirit', and we have taken note that the stories of Christ's conception and birth were intended to assert that in him God had entered into a new relation with the world.[8] At Christ's baptism, the Holy Spirit descends upon him in its fullness.[9] In Christian theology, therefore, the Holy Spirit must be understood in terms of Jesus Christ who fully manifested that Spirit in a human existence. It is little wonder, then, that the earliest Christians apparently made no distinction between the spirit of Jesus and the Holy Spirit. In St John's Gospel, Jesus promises his disciples that when he has gone from among them, they will not be left alone, for the Holy Spirit will come and will bring his words to their remembrance and lead them into truth.[10] Indeed, he will be 'a parallel figure to Jesus himself',[11] making present again their leader in their midst. And subsequent generations of disciples have ascribed to the inward testimony of the Holy Spirit their own experience of how, in the proclaiming of the word and the celebrating of the sacraments, the words and person of Jesus are again made present among his people.

Jesus' promise of the coming of the Spirit was fulfilled in that great 'inspiring' of the community which took place on the Feast of Pentecost. But this was also the fulfilling of the Old

Testament vision of a day when the Spirit would not be confined to heroes and prophets only, but would rest on the whole
people, conferring new life upon it. Peter in his sermon quoted
the prophet Joel: 'I will pour out my Spirit upon all flesh, and
your sons and your daughters shall prophesy, and your young
men shall see visions, and your old men shall dream dreams;
yea, and on my menservants and my maidservants in those days
I will pour out my spirit; and they shall prophesy.'[12] We remind
ourselves that no more than Abraham or Moses can Jesus
Christ be considered as an isolated individual. He is a public
figure, the focus of a community of people, indeed the centre of
a new humanity. His work in bringing into being a new
humanity succeeds to the extent that the characteristics of his
own existence become those of his community. If, then, the
Spirit of God descended on Jesus and lived fully in and with
him, this Spirit would have to stand in the same relation to the
new people of God, which would be a veritable community of
the Spirit. In effect, this means a community completely responsive to God, just as Jesus was completely responsive to the
Father. And the doctrine of the Holy Spirit helps us to understand better what this responsiveness is. For we have seen that
men use the word 'God' in respect of some experiences imping-
ing upon them and apparently originating in a source which
cannot be reduced to the level of any of the finite entities that
make up the world – experiences of grace, liberation, revelation,
opening up new horizons of self-understanding, and equally experiences of inner constraint and ultimate demand, summoning
to new depths of personal and communal being. These experiences are from beyond man, yet they also arise within him.
The Holy Spirit proceeds from God, yet the Holy Spirit is also
in the creation, striving in and with the creatures and bringing
them to the Father. We come back to the point that the Holy
Spirit is God in his nearness. This is God both within and without, God demanding and enabling our response.

Yet we must also understand the relation of the Holy Spirit
to human beings in such a way as does not infringe personal
existence, and the freedom that is an inalienable constituent of
personal existence. Sometimes the Holy Spirit has been conceived as an impersonal force which takes possession of men
and makes them do things of which they do not understand

themselves to be consciously the authors, as if they were puppets on a string. The action of the Holy Spirit, in such cases, is considered to be like the action of a drug. This would seem to be true of such apparently involuntary performances as the 'speaking with tongues', noted above. Admittedly, this did happen in the early church. But already Paul was making it clear in his letters that speaking with tongues was a somewhat dubious and dangerous way of manifesting possession by the Spirit. He himself lays great stress on the 'gifts' and 'fruits' of the Spirit. He acknowledges that there is great diversity of such gifts as from one individual to another and is willing to reckon among them prophecy, speaking with tongues and the like, but more important than these are the moral excellences, the greatest gifts of the Spirit – joy, peace, patience, kindness, hope and above all love.[13] These are the spiritual qualities seen in Christ, in whom the Spirit came in its fullness. We have seen that from the earliest times the awareness of God was closely associated with the moral demand.[14] The perfect response to God is the fulfilling of that demand, and it is through the grace of the Spirit that men in varying degrees can respond. But such a response is a free, personal response, not compelled but elicited; for these moral qualities have their value as they flow from free, creative, spiritual persons. Moral language would not be appropriate to robots or to human beings supposed to be spiritually 'possessed' in such a way that their words and actions were no longer under their conscious control.

The action of the Holy Spirit has been schematized in Christian theology, and certain traditional terms have been used to designate the moments of the Spirit's action – 'conviction of sin', 'election', 'justification', 'sanctification' and others. To be sure, no neat scheme can do adequate justice to a complex experience like the one we have in mind and, in particular, the moments do not clearly follow one another in succession, but may be all present together. Nevertheless, these traditional terms have their usefulness in helping us to understand the dynamics of life in the Spirit.

Conviction of sin may be considered first, for it is only as people become dissatisfied with themselves in their present condition that there can be any possibility of a turning or repentance, away from the present condition and into a new way of

life. The Spirit convicts of sin by confronting men with the
righteousness of Jesus Christ. We have seen that apart from
Christ man already has an awareness of the sin or disorder in
human affairs.[15] If he had no such awareness and, along with
it, an incipient dissatisfaction with his condition and a quest for
something better, then it is hard to see how he could ever
respond to the Holy Spirit at all. But if Christ is indeed the
fulfilment of the human possibility and the emergence of a
new humanity, then to be confronted with Christ and to see
him in that depth of significance which we ascribe to the work
of the Spirit, is to be convicted of sin in a quite new and pro-
found way. Especially the death of Christ reveals the horror of
man's fallen condition and the extent to which his life is
distorted.

But just as we have seen that in man's nature there are
affirmative forces as well as negative ones, so one cannot speak
of conviction of sin without at once speaking also of the affirmative action of the Spirit in choosing, calling, electing. Conviction of sin by itself would mean despair. But we are dealing here
with repentance, and repentance is simultaneously a turning
away and a turning toward. If to perceive Christ in the Spirit is
to be judged and convicted of sin, it is also to be drawn toward
him as that archetypal, fulfilled humanity to which man's
spiritual being, even in its sinful condition, obscurely testifies.
For if it did not, what possibility of response could there be, or
how could Christ mean anything to us? Admittedly, the notion
of election has sometimes been misunderstood in a deterministic fashion, as if it were simply an irresistible fate imposed
upon some men by a God who had laid down everything in
advance. One is indeed bound to think in that way, if one has
also concluded that human nature has been utterly shattered
by sin. But to follow that line of thought implies further that
God's action on men through his Spirit must be quite impersonal, treating them as automata without choice or responsibility. We have determined ourselves, however, to understand
the Spirit's action in not less than personal terms, for nothing
less would be worthy of spirit, whether the spirit of man or the
divine Spirit. The election and calling of the Spirit is indeed an
inward constraint, like the constraint which Abraham felt when
he went out from his home. But such constraint is an invitation,

not a compulsion, and it requires the response of a free act of commitment.

Justification does not mean that a man suddenly makes the transition from sin to righteousness. He may well find that a long painful journey still lies ahead of him. On the other hand, justification is not some kind of legal fiction, a pronouncing innocent or righteous in a purely forensic sense. In the theological sense, to be justified means to be drawn into the new humanity, to have conferred the dignity of belonging to the people of God, to be accepted in one's present condition as belonging to that people which is on its way to the righteousness of Christ. Thus justification is another aspect of the beginning of the new life of the Spirit.

Sanctification, on the other hand, is the deepening and development of the life which has begun in repentance election and justification. We have seen that this deepening and development consist primarily in bringing forth the gifts and fruits of the Spirit, and that the chief of these are moral qualities. The life of the Spirit is continuous with the natural morality belonging to all men, that drive toward a fuller humanity which, in spite of sin, still operates in all mankind. The Christian life in the community of the Spirit does not contradict natural morality but fulfils it and perhaps transforms it. For it sets man's moral strivings in a new context and opens up new horizons of the good. Specifically, in the Christian life man's moral endeavours are seen as response to the prior activity of God through his Spirit, and this can hardly fail to bring new hope and effort into the moral life. At the same time, man's aspiration toward a fuller personal humanity is made concrete and definite by being focused on Jesus Christ and the community which he inaugurated as the beginning of a new humanity.

Of all the Christian virtues, the highest is love. It is the most excellent of the gifts of the Spirit and the chief distinguishing mark of the community of the Spirit. It is very important, however, that such love should be understood in its full New Testament sense, and not trivialized, sentimentalized or voided of content. Love is not opposed to law but is, as Paul says, 'the fulfilling of the law'. Similarly, love is not opposed to justice, but requires justice as its instrument. The aim of love is full personal being for the beloved, and this is an aim that can be fulfilled only through thought and against a background of ordered social structures. Apart from these, love would degenerate to mere feeling and the Christian ethic would be reduced to sentimentalism.

It is also important to take full cognizance of the social, corporate dimension of the Christian ethic. Love is not to be understood only in individual terms. We have seen that love requires justice, but perhaps the social virtue which best expresses love is peace. Peace is love conceived in global terms; it shares with love the making possible of a fully personal existence for all within a free community. At this point we may recall that the quest of mankind for a higher and better mode of life has to be pursued both in terms of individual renewal and in terms of better social structures. In this connection we see still more clearly the important role that belongs to the people of God conceived as a community of the Spirit, for it is such a community of the Spirit that holds out to all men the concrete possibility of living together in peace with the maximum of human freedom, dignity and fulfilment.

Before we leave the theme of the Holy Spirit and its operation among men, there is another important theological point to be noted. This concerns the doctrine of God. We are now in a position to consider what is meant by the Christian belief in the triunity of God.[16]

Our lead into this doctrine has been afforded by our study of the community of faith, for this, though a single community, has shown itself to have a threefold aspect. We first met it as the people of God, continuous with that first people of God stemming from Abraham; then it became more concrete as the body of Christ, the visible community which came into being in solidarity with Christ and has continued to embody his life and work in the world; finally, it is the community of the Spirit, responding to God in the new way described in this chapter. But this triunity in the people reflects the triunity of God as he has made himself known to the people. A living dynamic God, like a person, is a diversity-in-unity. It is this mystery of the diversity-in-unity of God that the church seeks to express in her teaching of one God in three Persons. The Father is the ultimate self-subsistent reality, the primordial Being on whom all else depends; the Son or Word (for a word makes accessible the inward thought) is the agency whereby the hidden God emerges and makes himself known in a world of finite diversified creatures, so that we may call the Son the expressive Being; the Spirit flows from the Father through the Son into creation to sustain it in its relation to the Creator, so that Spirit is unitive Being.[17] Thus the doctrine of the triune God gathers up in summary form that knowledge of himself which God has given to his people.

Notes

1. Acts 1.11.
2. See above, p.9.
3. Acts 2.41.
4. See above, p.30.
5. See above, p.47.
6. Genesis 1.2
7. Ezekiel 37.1-14.
8. See above, p.59.
9. Mark 1.10.
10. John 14.26.

11. Rudolf Bultmann, *The Gospel of John: A Commentary*, Oxford: Blackwell, 1971, p.567.

12. Acts 2.17-18. Cf. Joel 2.28-29.

13. I Corinthians 12-13; Galatians 5.22-23.

14. See above, p.24.

15. See above, pp.32f.

16. See above, p.39.

17. For a fuller discussion, see my *Principles of Christian Theology*, London: SCM Press, 1966, chapter IX.

IX

The Signs of the People

We have seen that the people is the community of the Spirit, and we have learned something of the inward spiritual life of that community. But its life is by no means only inward or spiritual. The same people is the body of Christ. It exists as an embodied visible historical reality in the world, and so the fullness of its life emerges only as the inward spiritual springs of that life find expression in the community's dealings with the world and with society.

The Christian sacraments hold together in unity the inward and outward aspects of the people's life. In the familiar words of the Prayer Book, a sacrament is said to be 'an outward and visible sign of an inward and spiritual grace'. A sign is something public and manifest, yet something which always points beyond itself to what it signifies, in this case, the inward spiritual grace. However, a sacrament is more than a sign. Thus the Prayer Book declares further that sacraments 'are not only badges or tokens' but 'effectual signs', where the word 'effectual' implies that the sacraments do not simply represent a reality but are themselves a part of the reality, the vehicle by which the reality comes to be, the means by which God works. In personal and historical being, the inward and the outward are always in reciprocal interaction. To think of the inward as alone real is to miss the full range of personal being, reducing it to something ghostly and disembodied.

We have already seen that in the word of Scripture, as it is read and proclaimed in the community and its meaning attested by the Holy Spirit, God's acts of grace and revelation in Christ are renewed in the life of his people.[1] A similar renewing takes place in the celebration of the sacraments, but on a broader front. For the preached word is directed to the understanding and seeks to awaken the inward response of faith; while the sacraments address men both outwardly and inwardly, through the senses as well as through the understanding. It is a mistake to regard the sacraments as only another mode of proclaiming the word, with the visible action considered as merely a kind of visual aid. The sacraments all include, in one way or another, the ministry of the spoken word, but the sacramental action has more of a total character, addressing the whole man who is body and soul, spirit and sense, understanding and feeling and will. The ministry of the spoken word aims at instruction, but the sacramental ministry has total incorporation as its aim. But word and sacrament are not opposed to each other; they complement each other and have regard to the complex and many-sided being of man.

The word 'sacrament' is sometimes used in a very broad sense. Christ's life has been sometimes considered a sacrament, and obviously this is a possible way of thinking of it, for we have seen that his life was an earthly visible reality which yet revealed to the eye of faith a 'glory' in and beyond the immediately visible. The incarnation could thus be understood as a sacramental sign, and a highly effectual one. But it is better to think of Christ as the author of the sacraments rather than himself a sacrament, even the primary one. In recent years, many writers have discussed the church as a sacrament. Again, one can find good reasons for this. The church, as God's people in the world, is the sign of his kingdom already present, for, in spite of her imperfections, she points herself to the vision which she seeks to embody. But it is better to speak of the church as the bearer of signs and sacraments, than as itself a sacrament. One also sometimes hears the expression 'sacramental world', the whole creation being regarded as a sacrament. Our earlier discussions of natural theology and the doctrine of creation have made it clear that, for the Christian, the world finally does have a sacramental character. Yet we have also taken note of the ambiguous character of the world, and if we come to view it sacramentally, this happens because we have had the experience of some quite specific and concrete sacraments and have extended the sacramental outlook to the world as a whole.

Thus while we may acknowledge that on the one hand the

sacraments are rooted in the church and so in the incarnate life of Christ, and on the other that all creation can be regarded in a sacramental way, it is in the interests of clarity and precision to reserve the term 'sacraments' for those specific actions which have been traditionally so named in the Christian church. Two sacraments have been specially prized among almost all Christians, baptism and the eucharist, and, according to the New Testament, they were instituted by Christ himself. Certain other acts of a sacramental character have had their place in the church's life from the earliest times, and these also have been called 'sacraments' – the absolution of sins upon confession and repentance, the anointing of the sick, marriage, confirmation, ordination to the sacred ministy.

The gospels testify to the belief of the primitive church that Jesus himself had commanded his disciples not only to preach but to baptize 'in the name of the Father and the Son and the Holy Spirit' those who responded in faith to the preaching.[2] Of course, baptism had its antecedents in pre-Christian religion. Jesus himself had been baptized by John, but John's baptism is only one instance among many of the ritual use of water to signify a spiritual experience. Water, the outward sign used in baptism, has always been intimately related to human life and has gathered around itself a wealth of meaning. Early Christian theologians, looking back to the many references to water in the Old Testament, delighted to find in these prefigurings of baptism; and although such thoughts were not in the minds of the Old Testament writers, the universal symbolism of water in human experience made such allegorical interpretation easy and, within limits, legitimate. Thus the waters of chaos[3] from which God brought forth the ordered creation were compared to the waters of baptism from which arose the new creation, the new humanity in Christ; the purifying properties of water had long been associated with turning from sin to righteousness; and the life-sustaining power of water made it altogether appropriate that water should figure prominently in a rite designed to mark initiation into a new life.

The inward spiritual content to which baptism gives a visible expression are those experiences described in the last chapter[4] – the awakening of faith through the agency of the Holy Spirit. This awakening, we have seen, includes conviction of sin, the

turning in penitence from sin to a new life, the response of commitment to the calling of God and acceptance by God in Christ.
Baptism, we have said, gives outward visible expression to these
experiences, for they are not purely inward and private to the
individual concerned, but take place in embodied human existence through the public ministry of the church. Baptism is
incorporation into the people of God, and the outward aspect of
the sacrament is essential to its corporate character. Participation
in the new humanity of Christ cannot be separated from
participation in the new humanity of Christ's people. Here is
no private transaction between the individual soul and God, but
the receiving of the individual into the people of God where
alone he can become fully a person and a participant in the new
humanity. If we understand baptism – as Paul did[5] – as a dying
with Christ to the old life of sin and a rising with him into the
resurrection life of the Spirit (and this meaning was dramatically
portrayed in the primitive rite of baptism through the immersion
of the convert in the waters and his emergence as a new creature),
then his incorporation into Christ and his participation in the
life of Christ are to be understood not only in terms of an
inward relation to Christ but as outward visible participation in
Christ's people, which is his body.

In the early days of the church, those baptized were adults,
drawn from Jewish or pagan communities into the new Christian community. But soon the practice arose of baptizing the
children of Christian parents. The practice of infant baptism
has caused difficulties to some, because obviously a young child
has no explicit awareness of the meaning of baptism and cannot
at the time make that commitment of faith which is part of the
inward meaning. These difficulties arise, however, from understanding the sacrament in too individualistic a manner. If incorporation into the people of God is essential to the meaning
of baptism, then no human being is too young to receive it. It is
not necessary that he should explicitly understand it, but we
remember again that the sacraments, as operating on the whole
person, have effects that are not confined to what is understood.
Modern studies make it clear that children are deeply affected
from the very beginning by the personal environment in which
they grow up. They can be truly incorporated into Christ and
receive the Spirit long before they have any explicit understand-

ing of such matters, because they have been received in the threefold name into that people of God which is also the body of Christ and the community of the Spirit. But clearly all this lays a heavy responsibility on those who bring the child and those who receive him.

Although it is usually considered a distinct sacrament, confirmation can be understood only in close relation to baptism, and in the early church (and still in the Eastern church) baptism and confirmation were integrated in a single rite of initiation. Confirmation (or something like it) is very ancient. In the New Testament, we read that after Philip .the deacon had baptized some converts, apostles came down from Jerusalem and laid hands on them, whereupon they received the Holy Spirit.[6] The essence of the later theology and practice of confirmation is already present in this early incident.

The outward sign is the laying on of hands or anointing with chrism or both. The agent is the chief pastor (apostle or bishop) who either lays on hands in person or sends the chrism, and this connection of the sacrament with the chief pastor is highly important, for it makes clear that Christian initiation is not into a local congregation but into the people of God, the one church of all times and places, represented by the bishop. The inward grace is the receiving of the Holy Spirit, and since the presence of the Spirit is the mark of the mature Christian, confirmation has been understood as the sacrament of maturity and therefore as conferring full membership in the church.

It is important that confirmation should not be understood in any way that might seem to downgrade baptism. To say that the Holy Spirit is given in confirmation cannot mean that the Spirit is not also active in baptism or that his coming is instantaneous. In fact, part of the value of confirmation as distinct from baptism is simply that it shows that Christian initiation is not some magic instantaneous event, but a process taking time. This is especially true in Western practice, where confirmation comes only when the child has grown up and is able to participate personally in the community's commitment of faith. But whether baptism and confirmation are given together or separated by an interval of years, they must be understood theologically as embraced within a single action.

We pass to the eucharist. 'The Lord Jesus on the night when

he was betrayed took bread, and when he had given thanks, he broke it, and said, "This is my body, which is for you. Do this in remembrance of me." In the same way also the cup, after supper, saying, "This cup is the new covenant of my blood. Do this, as often as you drink it, in remembrance of me." [7] The outward signs are the bread and wine, and the fourfold action of taking, blessing, breaking and distributing. Like the water of baptism, bread and wine are substances intimately associated with human life and long invested with symbolic and religious significance. Now they become the vehicles of Christ's action and self-communication, for he is the bread of life[8] and the true vine.[9] The inward grace is the receiving of the reality of Christ, incorporation into him and into his people from whom he is inseparable. Whereas baptism and confirmation have to do with those acts of the Spirit whereby we are brought into the Christian life and therefore given once as signs of initiation, the eucharist may be regarded as the visible embodiment of the Spirit's continuing work of sanctification,[10] and so it is a sacrament which is received repeatedly and regularly.

The Christian eucharist is so packed with significance and has acquired such a central place in the life of the church that it is difficult to know where to begin in any description of it. Since, however, we are attempting to expound Christian theology with the people of God as the articulating idea, we begin from the fact that the eucharist is a meal, a social happening. The people eat and drink together and in this act (as in common meals from time immemorial) there takes place a realization and strengthening of the bonds of community, that which constitutes the people a people. But the people of God is no ordinary people, for it is constituted not by kinship or interest but by faith;[11] and therefore the meal is no ordinary meal, though it may light up hidden possibilities in all ordinary meals. Like so many of the other matters we have considered, the eucharist can be seen on two levels – there is the perceptible fact, the taking together of bread and wine, and there is the depth or glory to which this fact gives access, the realization of a true people of God in the body of Christ. For the eucharist points beyond itself. It recalls the presence of Christ with his disciples on the eve of his passion, and it also anticipates the heavenly banquet, symbolizing the completion of God's purposes for creation in the realization of a perfected community of peace and love. Thus the eucharist brings into the present both the remembered reality of the people's foundation in Christ and the anticipated reality of its final consummation, and so realizes here and now the new humanity in Christ.

We are saying then that what gives to the eucharistic meal its distinctive character is that it is focussed and founded in Christ, just as the people who celebrated the eucharist are likewise focussed and founded in Christ. The people have believed that in a unique way Christ is present with them in the eucharist. He is the president of the sacred banquet, yet it is also he who is received by the people so that they are incorporated into him and made one body, both with Christ and among themselves. The presence of Christ in the eucharist, not only in the consecrated bread and wine but in the words and actions, in the ministers of the eucharist and in the community as a whole, is above all to be understood as a personal presence. This presence has been expounded in various theories employing philosophical categories such as 'substance', 'significance', 'value', and so on, but its reality rests finally on the conviction that in the eucharist (as in the other sacraments and in the word) Christ, and therefore God in Christ, is still present and active among his people.

Since Christ is central to the eucharist and the eucharistic people, it is clear that the glory revealed in the eucharist is, like Christ's own glory, inseparable from sacrifice. In the eucharist, the bread and wine together with the people are offered in union with Christ to God, in the solemn recalling of his own death of self-giving love. We have seen that sacrifice was already a constitutive idea of the first people of God in its very beginnings under Abraham.[12] Self-giving was characteristic of God himself in his act of creation. In the history of creation, that self-giving came to its climactic moment in the incarnation and in Christ's giving himself up to death. The people of God can realize itself as that people only to the extent that sacrifice and self-giving has been taken into the very essence of its life. In the eucharist, the people recalls and identifies itself with the sacrifice of Christ, for only in this does its glory lie and its new humanity become manifest.

The remaining sacraments can be discussed more briefly. The absolution of the sins of the penitent, usually called the 'sacra-

ment of penance' or the 'sacrament of reconciliation', may, like
baptism and the eucharist, have been instituted by Christ himself. He claimed that 'the Son of man has authority on earth to
forgive sins'[13] and transmitted the same authority to the
apostles.[14] To be sure, this may be understood in the first
instance to refer to baptism. But baptism does not mean the end
of sin, and although baptism is given once only, the acts of
repentance and faith whereby one enters the Christian life have
often to be renewed within the community. The sacrament of
penance provides the appropriate means for this continuing
reconversion to Christ and the renewal of reconcilation. About
equally ancient is the anointing or unction of the sick. Although
we now know much more about disease, its causes and cures,
than men did in New Testament times, the bonds between body
and spirit remain mysterious. Health is far more than freedom
from germs, while salvation has in view the whole person, not
merely the soul. When we remember these facts, it is not surpris-
ing that this particular ministry to the sick has been widely
revived in recent times as an appropriate expression of the
people's concern to be present with and to strengthen those in
weakness or near to death. The institution of marriage has also
been considered by the people of God to have a sacramental
character. For marriage is the prototype of all human community – a community founded on love, yet not closed but open
and expanding into the family and beyond. This most natural
form of community still needs inward grace if it is to be perfected. Finally, there is the sacrament of orders, whereby some
members of the people of God receive special offices and respon-
sibilities within the people as a whole; but this will be discussed
in the next chapter, which deals with ministry.

At the beginning of this chapter, it was mentioned that for
the Christian the whole world has a sacramental character.
Taken in isolation, such a statement can be vague and somewhat
pantheistic. But once we have considered the specific sacraments
and how they touch the life of the people at so many points, we
can attach a more definite sense to the idea of a sacramental
universe. The specific sacraments of the people of God sensitize
its members in such a way that in material things, human situations, and historical events, they look for and perceive an
inward grace.

Notes

1. See above, p.15.
2. Matthew 28.19.
3. Genesis 1.2.
4. See above, pp.70ff.
5. Romans 6.1-11.
6. Act 8.14-17.
7. I Corinthians 11.23-25.
8. John 6.35.
9. John 15.1.
10. See above, p.72.
11. See above, p.11.
12. See above, p.21.
13. Mark 2.10.
14. Matthew 18.18; John 20.22-23.

X

The People in Ministry and Mission

Ministry and mission are two closely related characteristics of the people of God, and they are essential to it. They are among the basic 'givens' which make this people what it is, and without which it would be lacking something that is fundamental to its being as God's people. The four gospels are unanimous in testifying that Jesus committed a ministry to his followers, and that he sent them out on mission. But ministry and mission are intertwined. Those who first exercised the Christian ministry became known as 'apostles', men who were 'sent', while 'mission' also means simply 'sending'. At the commissioning of his disciples, Jesus says: 'As the Father has sent me, even so I send you.'[1] There is a parallel between God's sending his Son, and Christ's sending his people. The ministry and mission of the people have their origin in Christ and are indeed extensions of his own ministry and mission. Preaching, teaching, healing, exorcising, absolving – whatever Jesus had done, we find the apostles and their associates doing in the days after Pentecost; but there are differences, for Jesus himself, and especially his death and resurrection, have become the main theme of the preaching, and those who respond are baptized into his name.

We begin with the idea of ministry. We have seen how the role of ministry was by no means foreign to the first people of God, for very early in the history of that people we find it exercising a priestly function in relation to the cities of the plain, while in its time of maturity we find the prophetic interpretation of the people as the servant of the Lord, bringing justice to the nations.[2] These ways of understanding the role of

the people receive a new depth of fulfilment when we come to
Jesus Christ, represented in the New Testament as the 'high
priest' who has gathered up in his work all priestly ministry,[3]
and likewise as the servant who has emptied himself even to
the extent of the cross for the sake of his reconciling mission.[4]
The ministry passes in turn to the new people of God. This
people can be described as a 'royal priesthood',[5] and their vocation is to serve as Christ had served.[6]

It is clear from these remarks that what is fundamental to
any understanding of ministry and priesthood are the ministry
and priesthood of Christ himself, as both fulfilment and arche-
type. All Christian ministry is participation in Christ's ministry.
It is clear also that Christian ministry belongs in the first
instance to the whole people of God, for the whole people is
incorporated by baptism into Christ and therefore shares in his
saving ministry. This corporate ministry of the whole people is
stressed by the use in the New Testament of the collective noun:
the people constitutes a 'royal priesthood'. Expressions such as
'ministers and people', though commonly used, must be reck-
oned unfortunate, for they obscure the fact that the ministers
themselves belong to the people of God, and that the whole
people has a ministry. There are indeed differences between
clergy and laity – and a lay theology is misunderstood if it turns
into an anti-clerical theology[7] – but these differences are very
badly expressed when one talks of the church as made up of
'ministers and people'. All constitute one people, and all share
in the one ministry of Christ. On the other hand, however, one
must declare that equally unfortunate are such expressions as
'the priesthood of all believers'. This is far too individualistic a
way of understanding the priesthood which belongs collectively
to the whole people and is a corporate priesthood, not to be
divided up in some supposedly egalitarian way.

We are driven back to the idea of a 'people' and to the difficult problem of the relation of the corporate and individual
aspects of human existence. A people is not a mob or a crowd
or a mere sum of individuals. It has a structure which, for want
of a better name, we may call 'organic', though the structure
of a people is more subtle than that of an organism. Abraham
and his companions, and also Christ and his disciples, show us
the structure of a people as a diversity in unity, a social entity

with a centre and a leadership. The new people, the church, has been structured from the beginning. The twelve, deriving their ministry directly from Christ, and with them their ever-widening circle of associates, constituted a single people, but a people in which there was diversity of function and of office and even of authority. Indeed, if all had been assimilated to one type, there would never have been a people, properly so called, but only a crowd. The other New Testament images of the church make it clear that this is a true community and embraces diversities within a centred unity. The people is the body of Christ, and this way of speaking explicitly introduces the organic metaphor. A body is a unity, but its unity and efficient function-ing depend on the members each performing the special work for which each is fitted. As Paul points out, not all are apostles or prophets or teachers. There is a diversity of gifts, and this is necessary to the well-being of the body as a whole.[8] If we think of the people as the community of the Spirit, the same message comes through. The freedom and dignity of the life in the Spirit are not realized in unmitigated individualism. 'For God is not a God of confusion but of peace ... All things should be done decently and in order.'[9]

The diverse forms of ministry within the people cannot be supposed to be in rivalry with one another. They are needed *in their diversity* if the ministry of the whole people is to be rich and comprehensive. In times of clerical domination, the ordained ministries have enjoyed such prestige that the ministry of the laity has been obscured and neglected. But it would be equally mistaken to think that the ministry of the laity (a ministry which is itself very diverse) can only assert itself by seeking to assimilate those functions which have been traditionally re-served to the ordained ministries. Such assimilation would rest on a misunderstanding of the lay ministry and would divert it from its proper goals. The all-important ministry of the whole people can be exercised with full effect only when it gathers up in a harmonious unity the widest possible range of differing ministries.

That all-important ministry of the whole people is called by Paul the ministry of reconciliation.[10] All ministry must have this goal of reconciliation in view, and reconciliation is in turn to be interpreted in terms of Christ's own reconciling or atoning work. Reconciliation implies a condition of humanity in which persons live together in peace, freedom, dignity, love and mutual helpfulness, and this is at the same time the glorifying of God because his creation will have been rescued from the alienation of sin, brought to the fulfilment for which it is destined, and so reconciled to himself.

Within the total ministry of the people, the special ordained ministries have their distinctive place. In the earliest days of the people, the apostles constituted a nucleus. They provided the leadership and were the principal preachers and spokesmen. They had been witnesses of Jesus' career,[11] but too much stress should not be laid on this point, for, as Kierkegaard pointed out, those who actually saw and conversed with Jesus enjoyed no advantage over the disciples of later times, for what is important here is not seeing with the eyes but that seeing in faith which is a beholding of Jesus in his ultimate significance, his 'glory'.[12] When the first apostles began to die out, they appointed new men to take over their work. Thus there continued in the church a ministry in succession to that of the apostles – a succession both in the truth of the apostolic doctrine and in a visible personal community. Within a few generations, this Christian ministry was to be found throughout the inhabited world of those days, wherever the people of God had penetrated. Every principal city had its bishop, and with him were associated presbyters and deacons. Through the ministry of word and sacraments, those officers of the people promoted the mission and nurtured the life of the people itself, and they have continued to render their service in the subsequent history of the people.

But we remember that ministry belongs to the whole people. For a long time, the ordained ministries were emphasized to such an extent that they came to be regarded as the only forms of Christian ministry. But in recent times the ministry of the laity has been rediscovered. This rediscovery has perhaps been due above all to the secularization of society. The ministry of word and sacraments, carried on in churches and Christian congregations, is often far from 'where the action is' in the contemporary world. There are many areas of our society where only the layman penetrates and where only he, with his specialized training as economist, banker, medical man, sociologist or whatever it may be, really understands the problems. A lively lay apostolate is essential if the people of God is to minister to contemporary society.

We must not think, however, of an ordained ministry and a lay ministry going on side by side. They belong together in the total ministry of the people, and must be in constant interaction. If we grasp the truly corporate character of the people, then we must appreciate also the corporate character of ministry. Christian ministry is most effectively done not by individuals but by teams, and teams which include both lay and clerical members. Within the team, there is, of course, division of labour. Each member supplies his contribution to the whole, and the contribution of each differs. If all wanted to do the same things, then we would not have a team but an amorphous assemblage of individuals. The practical organization of ministry will vary greatly from one situation to another, and the patterns will no doubt change frequently as society itself changes. However, the basic theological principles governing this changing situation are those already noted at an early stage of our inquiry into the people of God – collegiality, concelebration and, not least, co-theologizing.

From ministry we turn to the closely related idea of mission. It was the intensely missionary spirit of Christianity that sent the first disciples out from Jerusalem to the furthest parts of the Graeco-Roman world, and that at later stages of history caused the spread of the people to the furthest continents so that today the Christian faith is established in almost every part of the globe, even if only very precariously in some areas. Yet the whole idea of mission has been undergoing a crisis in recent years. The older conception of mission as the visible expansion of the church with the goal of making it a global society has sharply declined. This was, however, the conception of mission that had operated with variable degrees of vigour and success for something like nineteen centuries. But the idea of mission has not been abandoned. A new and more fluid conception has emerged. The new conception of mission is as much interested in those areas where Christianity has long flourished as the majority religion (so-called 'Christendom') as it is in those parts of the world where the majority of the people belong to non-Christian religions, for the Christianity of the secularized nations of the West is little more than nominal as far as great masses of the people are concerned. At the same time, the explicit conversion of non-Christians to the Christian faith and their incorporation into the church is given much less prominence in the new concept of mission than it had in the old. Where preaching, baptizing and setting up new communities of the faithful were once seen as the primary goals of mission, these tend today to be regarded as secondary matters, indeed, almost as matters of indifference. The goal of mission is conceived instead in terms that are largely secular or even political, namely, the provision of conditions that will enable a truly human life for those who are at present deprived of it, whether in the industrial countries of 'Christendom' or in the undeveloped regions of the earth. The church is the self-effacing servant in these situations, and is seen by some missiologists as itself a marginal institution which will frequently work through other institutions (or encourage those whom it reaches to work through other institutions) for the achievement of its goals, rather than making itself the centre of operations.

It is true that this new understanding of mission can become exaggerated to the point at which the church becomes just another social agency and loses its distinctive character as the people of God. It is true also that the process of secularization has penetrated into the church itself, so that traditional beliefs which were once powerful motives to mission have come to be doubted or are held in a more tentative way; and likewise traditional Christian values have been overshadowed by the values current in societies that are frankly devoted to the production and consumption of material goods. Alistair Kee has justly pointed out that today it is often the church (or its agencies) 'which conceives of solutions to human problems in purely economic terms'.[13]

As well as the secularization of beliefs and values within the church, one must also take note of the revulsion against triumphalism. Mission, it is now believed, has been in the past too closely concerned with the aggrandisement of the ecclesiastical institution. The motive of expansion has been allowed too much scope at the expense of the motive of service. Furthermore, such expansion has often been closely associated with the imperialistic thrust of the Western nations. Whatever the selflessness and devotion of Christian missionaries may have been (and assuredly they have been great), it can hardly be denied that the path to mission was sometimes opened up by soldiers and traders who were neither selfless nor devout, and that Christian missions were not unwilling to utilize openings so provided.

These are practical considerations that have affected the understanding of mission. At some points they are justified, at others they are certainly questionable. But there are also theological considerations, and a brief discussion of these will make clearer the contemporary mission of the church and will also guard against the kind of exaggeration that would turn the Christian mission into a purely secular effort for social and political improvement of the human lot.

These theological considerations are to be seen in the light of the concept of the people of God, as we have come to understand it in the earlier part of this book. We recall that the people of God stands in a dialectical relation to the world at large.[14] The people was founded by an act of separation, and unless it maintained its distinctiveness, it would possess neither interest nor importance. Yet even in its separateness the people remains bound to the whole human race, and its distinctive calling is for the sake of all. This dialectic of separation and solidarity is of the highest importance for the understanding of mission. The church is not (as some ages have thought of it) an ark floating on the stormy seas, so that all who would be saved must be brought aboard while the wicked world perishes around. But neither may the church simply identify with the world, as some advocates of a secular Christianity seem to argue today. Rather, as I have said before, the people of God has 'blurred edges'. Its distinctive life as a people *of God* causes it to stand out from the world as a focus and centre of a life which the world at large does not know. Yet the fact that it is a *people* of God points to its solidarity with all people and reminds us that ideally all people are the people of God, for he created them all and their true end is in him.

If one held to the 'ark' idea of the church, then it would be an overwhelmingly urgent task to bring everyone aboard the ark (that is to say, explicitly into the baptized community) for there alone would be salvation. But if we grasp the paradox of separation and solidarity, with its accompanying conception of blurred edges, then it will not seem so imperative that all should be brought explicitly into the Christian fellowship. For the people's solidarity with all men as the focus and representative of a true humanity means that none are quite cut off from it. Especially, Christians ought gladly to recognize the role of those who, under whatever name or sign, are following in the ways of truth and righteousness and seeking a fuller humanity for themselves and others. They are to be found in other world-religions, and also among those who do not profess any religion. Such people should not be called 'anonymous Christians', as sometimes happens. They are to be accepted as Buddhists, Jews, humanists or whatever they are. But their kinship with Christians is to be recognized, and the lines that separate us are blurred at many points. Dialogue and co-operation with such people is possible, for the sake of ends which they and Christians have in common. Of course, Christians hope that in the course of such dialogue and co-operation, many will be drawn into the full explicit fellowship of the people of God and that their life and labours will be deepened and enlarged by such definite incorporation into the body of Christ. But Christians today also recognize in a way that nineteenth-century Christians usually did not that the people's mission of glorifying God by leading his human creatures into a fuller and deeper personal and communal life implies many tasks besides making converts, and that in our time at least some of these other tasks may take precedence. All Christians pray and long for the consummation when Christ will be all and in all, but they also have the wisdom to recognize the relative and provisional character of every actual situation. This also explains why, at the present time, the practical and secular aspects of mission will bulk more largely than at some other times. For the Christian mission is directed to bringing fuller life to mankind, as indeed Christ himself was sent 'that they may have life, and have it abundantly'.[15] In a world where many millions lack the basic material conditions which must be fulfilled before there can be freedom, dignity and peace, mission may well begin with these basic material things, and this is already a tacit obedience to and proclamation of him who came to give life.

But the Christian knows, too, that *abundant* life is not to be found in material things alone. The fullness of life for which man is destined has a transcendent dimension. There can be no truly Christian mission that is not conjoined with prayer, and it is to the prayer of the people of God that we must next turn our attention.

Notes

1. John 20.21.
2. See above, pp.21-25.
3. Hebrews 4-8.
4. Philippians 2.5-11.
5. I Peter 2.9.
6. John 13.12-17.
7. See above, p.5.
8. I Corinthians 12.
9. I Corinthians 14.33 and 40.
10. II Corinthians 5.18.
11. Acts 2.21-22.
12. S. Kierkegaard, *Philosophical Fragments*, tr. David F. Swenson, Princeton: Princeton University Press, 1936, p.44.
13. Alistair Kee, *The Way of Transcendence*, London: Penguin Books, 1971, p.219.
14. See above, p.19.
15. John 10.10.

XI

The Prayer of the People

The people of God is a praying people. Prayer is just as much a 'given' of the people's life as mission, for that life is focussed in Jesus Christ and it is clear that prayer had an essential place in his own life and that he commended the practice to his followers. At the end of the last chapter we took note that although ministry and mission will not neglect the material needs of men, they cannot become purely secular activities, for their roots are in prayer and, more than that, the abundant life which the people proclaims is a life with a transcendent dimension. The whole exposition of the people of God in this book has brought us to a point where we can readily recognize the truth and importance of the following words of Douglas Jones: 'Many false turns will be taken unless it is realized that the church exists not only to be the servant of Christ to the world, to speak God's word and bring life to men, but also, as anticipating the perfect life of the kingdom, to articulate the *response* of creation to the Creator. Worship therefore is as important as mission.'[1] The same writer points out that the church has always a twofold character – its servant character as it ministers to the needs of men, and its hidden glory as it anticipates here and now the new creation in which humanity is perfectly at one with God.[2]

Of course, prayer and mission are not in any sense rivals, as if they competed with one another for our time and energy. It is hard to see how mission could be sustained or how it could have direction if there were not times of prayer when one disengages oneself from the immediate activity in order to engage in a different way with the constraining reality of the one who has sent his people on mission. Prayer strengthens mission, and it

brings hope and illumination to the many tasks of mission by
relating them to a single vision. If mission needs prayer to
strengthen and direct it, prayer needs mission to realize it.
Prayer cannot be just cultivation of the inner life, for if it is
true prayer, it takes place in the most sensitive awareness of the
surrounding world and its needs, and must lead into whatever
action is possible for responding to these needs.

But these remarks do not mean that prayer is only instru-
mental to mission. Prayer is both a means to mission and the
end of mission. Prayer is a means because, as we have seen, it
strengthens and illuminates the Christian task. But prayer is
also the end, for mission itself aims at bringing abundant life
to men, and this in turn implies that human life is made open
to the reality of God and finds its fulfilment in a transcendent
communion which is prayer at its highest. Prayer and worship
strengthen for the tasks of mission in every actual historical
situation in which the people finds itself; but in the end, when
the tasks of mission are done and the kingdom of God is a
completed reality, prayer and worship will remain as the new
community celebrates its being in God and with God. 'Behold,
the dwelling of God is with men. He will dwell with them, and
they shall be his people, and God himself will be with them.'³
This close communion with God and with his people is both the
end of the people's pilgrimage and the highest reach of prayer.

But we turn our minds from this vision of the end back to our
actual situation in the present. What is the place of prayer here
and now? To many people, it appears that prayer has become
discredited in the modern world. Has not prayer been utilized
as a kind of magic for the manipulation of events, and have we
not learned that control over the world is to be achieved not
through prayer but through our own efforts, in work, in science,
and in the application of scientific knowledge? Thus to many
people prayer has come to look like a superstitious survival, or
as the refuge of weak minds when all other avenues are closed.
In an earlier discussion,⁴ we have seen that God himself appears
redundant in the modern world, and the objections brought
against belief in God would hold in a similar way against
prayer. And just as we were bound to acknowledge that much
of the critique of God has its measure of validity against some
of the traditional ideas of God, so we must acknowledge that

much that has passed for prayer has been infected with magical ideas and egotistical desires. Yet in spite of all the criticism, even the justified criticism, prayer remains a very deep instinct in human life and one is constantly astonished at the ways in which prayer reasserts itself in our secularized society. And as well as explicit prayer, there are practices near to prayer, practices of meditation and contemplation that are valued by people of no religious faith.

Obviously the whole question of prayer is tied in very closely with the understanding of God. Prayer is address; it is language directed toward God. But who is this God to whom our prayer is addressed? The discredited forms of prayer are those which are infected by magical ideas and egotistical motives or which try to use prayer as a shortcut to results that can only be achieved by toil and effort. These mistakes in turn imply a mistaken idea of God. The false understanding of prayer rests on a false understanding of God – that false understanding of God as an absolute celestial monarch, able to act arbitrarily in the affairs of the world but himself unaffected by what goes on there.[5] If God is understood (or misunderstood) in such a way, then prayer, too, is misunderstood and can easily become an attempt to enlist the divine favour, to secure that God is on our side and carries out our wishes. To put the matter so bluntly is perhaps to caricature popular prayer, yet there is some truth in the caricature. If, on the other hand, we recognize that God and the world stand in a much more intimate relation, taking seriously God's immanence in the world as well as his transcendence of it, and acknowledging that a creation, especially a creation including free finite agents, is bound to be experienced as a self-limitation on the part of the Creator, then our whole understanding of prayer changes. Prayer can no longer have anything to do with influencing or bending the divine will in accordance with our desires, but rather with bending our wills to God's will, so that the hindrances that stand in his way are removed and his good purposes for his creatures given free course. When we recall what has been said above about the Holy Spirit,[6] we shall understand too that our prayer to God is not only our address to him but is also his prayer in us. Prayer is therefore the establishing of a communion between God and the finite agents such as will enable these agents to work with

God for the fulfilment of his creation. In such prayer, there is nothing either magical or egotistical, but it can certainly be a dynamic transforming force in the world.

Surely this understanding of prayer receives confirmation when we look at that model of Christian prayer, the Lord's Prayer. When the disciples asked Jesus to teach them to pray, he gave them a pattern which remains as a criterion for all subsequent prayer.[7] 'Our Father who art in heaven, hallowed be thy name.' The beginning of prayer is the recognition of the reality of God, the unseen creative holy mystery from which everything derives its being. 'Thy kingdom come, thy will be done on earth as it is in heaven.' There is no request for our wishes to be fulfilled, but for God's will to be done, for his will contains every worthy desire that we could ever entertain, and his kingdom fulfils every right aspiration that could ever enter our minds. 'Give us this day our daily bread.' There is nothing egotistical in this simple request, no hint of concupiscence; it is an expression of trust in him who is the source and sustainer of our lives. 'And forgive us our debts, as we have forgiven our debtors.' This is an acknowledgement both of our failure to play our part as we should in the enterprise of creation, and of the emptiness of any atonement with God which is not matched by our active seeking to be at one with our neighbours. 'And lead us not into temptation, but deliver us from evil.' All human life is threatened by temptation and evil, so the prayer ends with the request for the divine grace to strengthen us in our human weakness.

Not only the Lord's Prayer but the great common prayers of the church serve as a norm. Prayers can be classified as public or private. Public prayer takes place in the eucharistic liturgy and on such other occasions of common prayer as the people of God comes together to hear his word, to praise and thank him, to make confession of sin, to ask him for grace and whatever else is necessary to the people's life. Private prayer takes place in the life of the individual believer, and it obviously has a more fluid and *ad hoc* character as it is related to his peculiar needs and changing situations. Almost inevitably, public prayer assumes set liturgical forms, while private prayer may be quite informal. We say, however, that the common prayers of the church are a norm by which private prayers are to be measured.

Here again we come to the relation between the corporate and individual aspects of Christianity. Both are needed. But in prayer,
as in other matters, the individual is all too easily carried away
by his own wishes and idiosyncrasies, and these have to be kept
in check by ensuring that private prayer is always kept in
relation to the prayer of the whole church and is compatible
with those great prayers in which the church has expressed its
corporate mind. This need not for a moment stifle the spon-
taneity of prayer, but it does help to safeguard against those
distortions which can so easily occur and which then bring
prayer into disrepute.

Prayer is of many kinds and takes place on many levels. Some
forms come more naturally than others, and some are learned
only through long training and practice. Among the kinds of
prayer are petition, including intercession; thanksgiving; confession; meditation; contemplation. This list is by no means
exhaustive, but if we consider briefly the kinds of prayer mentioned, we shall be able to understand better what prayer is
and how great is the range of prayer.

We begin with petition, which is probably the simplest and
commonest form of prayer. 'Petition' means simply asking, and
indeed the word 'prayer' itself means asking. Precisely because
petition is asking, this is the kind of prayer that most easily
falls into the dangers of becoming selfish or magical, as described above. We tend to ask for what we want, without paus-
ing to consider whether we ought to want it or whether our
neighbours want it or indeed whether God might be supposed
to want it. If this kind of prayer is to be used rightly, we need
also to engage in other forms of prayer of a more meditative
kind, such as will lead us to a fuller understanding of the Christian relevation of God. We must then let our petitions be controlled by what we have learned of God. We shall then ask for
ourselves or for others only what is consonant with God's will
for his creatures, so far as we know it, in the confidence that
what he wills for them is better than anything they could desire
apart from him.

We sometimes hear the question: if God already knows what
is good for his creatures, then what is the point of asking for
anything in prayer? The question rests on the mistaken sup-
position that prayer is intended to bend or cajole God into will-

ing something, whereas, as we have seen, the point is rather that we may will with God and work with God. He already wills what is good, but his will is hindered and frustrated by those imperfect and often evil finite wills to which he has granted freedom. Only when these finite wills have freely aligned themselves with his will can his good purposes be fulfilled.

So far we have been discussing petition in general, but it is necessary to say something about that particular form of petition which we call 'intercession' – those prayers for others in which it is asked that they may be healed of sickness or that they may be preserved in peace or that they may respond to the needs of someone else, or whatever it may be. This is an ancient form of Christian prayer, and it usually has an important place in the course of the celebration of the eucharist. But many people now have intellectual problems about intercessory prayer. If, on the one hand, we are to think of our universe as virtually self-regulating, and if, on the other hand, we are to abandon the thought of God as an exalted monarch, beyond or above the world though able to intervene in its affairs, how is it possible to justify the practice of intercessory prayer?

I do not think that many Christians would be satisfied with what may be called the 'reductionist' explanation of such prayer. According to this view, the benefit of the prayer accrues to the person who prays. The prayer makes him more compassionate and more sensitive in perceiving the needs of others. Of course, it may benefit them indirectly also, by spurring action on their behalf. Now this reductionist explanation is true so far as it goes, and the Christian will readily agree that 'compassionate thinking'[8] has value in itself. But Christians have always believed that intercessory prayer does more. It brings the creative and healing power of God himself into the situation. On the account of the world and of human life given in the earlier chapters of this book, it is surely possible to believe this. The world is no mere physical world, but one informed by the creative Spirit of God. It is no merely deterministic world, for it contains free personal agents. Furthermore, these agents are bound together by many ties, so that what happens to one can hardly fail to affect another. With this understanding of our world – a Christian understanding – we can see that prayer provides, so to speak, openings into this closely woven mesh so that the divine Spirit may enter the situation. And his action, let us remember,[9] is in no sense magical, but thoroughly personal.

Let us leave petition, and consider prayers of confession and thanksgiving. It is convenient to take these two together. They arise simply through our confrontation with the goodness of God in Christ. That this goodness has appeared and borne fruit in a world where so much is ambiguous or even bad is, to the people of God, a never ending cause for thanksgiving. The prayer of confession is the converse of this. It is the people's acknowledgement in the face of God of their failure to engage themselves wholly in the way of life to which they have been called and of their many fallings away. So these prayers of thanksgiving and confession define and deepen the people's relation to God and promote the continual renewal of the people's dedication to him in the Holy Spirit.

Meditation is usually understood as the kind of prayer in which we let the mind dwell on some of the great truths or affirmations of the Christian faith so that these, as it were, sink into us and become part of us. Frequently the material for meditation is scriptural – the biblical teaching about God or the biblical narratives of his dealings with men. Obviously the eucharist, at a recalling of the passion of Christ, has, among many other dimensions, a meditative one. The daily offices, built as they are on the psalms, the scriptures and the framework of the Christian year, provide a major resource for meditation on the contents of the faith. The rosary is a popular form of meditation on the mysteries of the gospel. At the opposite end of the scale, theology itself may be considered as the most sophisticated kind of meditation, for it is the reflective attempt to understand as fully as possible and to assimilate the meaning of the Christian religion. The aim of meditation is immersion in the substance of Christian faith, so that it shapes the life and thinking of the people of God. Thus meditation is part of the process of sanctification, the maturing of the people toward that fulfilled humanity which always lies ahead of their actual condition.

There is no end to the explorations carried out in meditative prayer. Yet we can distinguish still another level of prayer. Whereas meditation uses words and dwells on particular ideas or stories, there is a form of prayer which simply keeps silence before God. This is contemplation. But we would misunderstand the silence of contemplative prayer if we thought that such prayer has no content. Rather, in contemplation all the moments of prayer are gathered up in a fullness which no words can adequately express. If indeed the final goal of the people of God is to enjoy his immediate presence in its completeness, then contemplation is a foretaste of this goal in the midst of the world.

This chapter has given us an idea of the central importance of prayer in the life of the people of God. It is prayer that illuminates the goal of the people and gives direction to its mission. It is prayer that supplies the inward strength and serenity so that the people persists in its mission even through great adversities. This prayer takes many forms, and although all of them contribute to the life of the people, it is not necessary that every member of the people should cultivate all the forms of prayer. In prayer, as in other matters, there will be a diversity within the unity. But it is important that each member of the people should consider seriously what his contribution to the prayer of the people should be, and work out for himself a discipline in which he uses those forms of prayer that are most helpful to him and best enable him to be an effective member of the whole body.

Notes

1. Douglas R. Jones, *Instrument of Peace: Biblical Principles of Christian Unity*, London: Hodder & Stoughton, 1965, p.22.
2. Ibid. p.57.
3. Revelation 21.3.
4. See above, pp.36f.
5. See above, p.49.
6. See above, p.69.
7. Matthew 6.7-15.
8. Cf. John Macquarrie, *Paths in Spirituality*, London: SCM Press, 1972, pp.27ff.
9. See above, p.69.

XII

The End of the People

In this final chapter, we consider the all-important question of how it will all end. When we talk of the 'end' of the people, the expression can be understood in at least two ways. We may think of 'end' in the sense of goal, and our foregoing discussions have made clear the kind of goal at which the people aims. It is the goal of a new humanity, in which the quality of life manifested in Jesus Christ will be manifested in all men. But we can also think of 'end' in the sense of a final state. What will be the final state of the people of God? Will they just fade out of history, as so many other peoples have done? Or will this people, and with it the whole human race, perish in some cosmic catastrophe, and will the universe then continue on its unseeing way as if they had never been? No doubt these are possibilities, and some may think they are almost certainties. But the faith of the people is that its end, in the sense of its final state, will coincide with its end, in the sense of its goal—that it will not cease to be until it has led all mankind into the new society of peace, dignity and freedom. This faith is based not on what the people possesses in itself (for it acknowledges its own failures to realize the new humanity) but in the fact that it is a people called and destined by God, and in that sense indefectible:[1] 'The powers of death shall not prevail against it.'[2] This is the eschatological hope, the hope concerning the last things, where the 'last things' means the ultimate destiny not only of the people of God but of the whole human race and, indeed, of the cosmos.

An eschatological hope was implicit in the people of God from the very beginning. When the first people of God led by Abraham went out from their Mesopotamian city into the

desert, they were not going out into nothing, but responding to
a call that promised them a fuller being. It was for this that they
hoped. As time went on, the eschatological hope became more
explicit. For a long time that hope was frankly this-worldly in
character. It was the hope of an earthly kingdom under an ideal
ruler who would ensure justice, peace and material prosperity,
though, to be sure, he would also uphold true religion and
nurture the spiritual life of the people. But this hope was dis-
appointed,[3] and as it faded more and more from the realm of
practical possibility, some became convinced that one must look
beyond the relativities and contingencies of world-history, and
a new and more radical kind of eschatological hope was born.
This was the apocalyptic expectation of late Judaism, that the
present world order would be radically transformed into a new
order, and that this would happen not by human striving but
by the action of God. Of course, a cynic might say that the Jews
were driven into the realm of apocalyptic fantasy through the
failure of their more sober hopes and their inability to accept
this failure as the falsification of their beliefs. On the other
hand, it could be argued that the Jewish apocalyptists had
learned to see more subtly into the hope of the people and that
there are important insights in their teaching, though these are
covered up by the apocalyptic imagery and mythology.

In any case, Jewish apocalyptic was flourishing at the time of
the origin of Christianity, and many of its ideas were taken over
by the new people of God. We have already noted that Jesus
himself seems to have believed that the end of the age was
imminent,[4] and this belief was shared by Paul[5] and other leaders
of the new community. Recent New Testament scholarship
has emphasized and perhaps even overemphasized the thoroughly eschatological character of the primitive Christian community
and its teaching. Nineteenth-century scholars tended to mod-
ernize and rationalize New Testament teaching, and to play
down anything in it which is incompatible with a modern outlook. But this is to misrepresent the New Testament. Johannes
Weiss was the first of a series of scholars to show that 'Jesus'
idea of the kingdom of God appears to be inextricably involved
with a number of eschatological-apocalyptical views' and that
'the real difference between our modern world-view and that of
primitive Christianity is that we do not share the eschatological

attitude' but 'pass our lives in the joyful confidence that *this* world will become more and more the showplace of the people of God'.[6] Schweitzer, Barth, Bultmann and, more recently, Moltmann are theologians of the present century who have all stressed the eschatological character of the New Testament message. They have done this in different ways, for there are different possibilities of interpretation. But they are all agreed that the eschatological elements in the New Testament are too central for us to sweep them under the carpet in order to make the New Testament message 'acceptable' to the modern mentality. In fact, the strangeness and even offensiveness of the eschatological has to be asserted so that Jesus, too, can be seen in his otherness and transcendence and not be reduced to the dimensions which our culture (or any culture) seeks to impose upon him.

But let us look more closely for a moment at the New Testament teaching on the last things. In its early form, this teaching was that the present world and its history would come to an end in the very near future. God, through the agency of the heavenly Son of Man, would judge the human race. The righteous would dwell with God for ever in a new kingdom of heaven, while the wicked would be cast into outer darkness. But events did not happen that way. The first generation of Christian disciples was dying out, and still the Son of Man did not come on the clouds to inaugurate the new age. Perhaps some regarded this failure as falsifying Christianity, and fell away, just as members of the first people had fallen away when their expectations seemed to be falsified.[7] Certainly, there are late passages in the New Testament which make it clear that there were doubts and questionings in the mind of the Christian community.[8] Some reconsideration of eschatological doctrine was demanded. Broadly speaking, we may say that two moves were open. One might still look for an end of the world, but now postponed to an indefinite time in the future; or one might claim that the eschatological events were already taking place in the present. Actually these alternatives are not quite exclusive of each other. In the Gospels of Matthew, Mark and Luke the eschatological events are still conceived as lying in the future, and yet at the same time it is believed that the kingdom of God is already breaking in. But in the Gospel of John, generally supposed to be the latest of the gospels and so as coming from a time when hopes of an early end to the age were fading, the eschatological events are almost wholly brought into the present: 'Now is the judgment of this world!'[9] Yet it would be difficult to maintain that even in this gospel the thought of a future end has been quite given up.

The two possible ways of interpreting eschatology found in the New Testament are, in the main, still the alternatives that confront theology today. And now, as then, it is difficult to believe that one of them can be taken as adequate without some acknowledgement of the truth in the other. Indeed, their disjunction conceals in itself a fundamental tension that has kept reappearing throughout our study – the tension between individual and community. On the whole, the interpretation of eschatology as something that has already happened or is now in process of happening (the view sometimes called 'realized' eschatology) lends itself very well to the question of the final destiny of the individual but not nearly so well to the question of the final destiny of the community or the race. This would seem to demand some kind of futuristic eschatology. We have, of course, maintained throughout this book that any adequate account of Christianity – or even of humanity in general – must take cognizance of both the individual and corporate dimensions. But in taking the people of God as the articulating concept of theology, we have deliberately stressed the corporate aspect, believing that it is appropriate to do so at the present time.

Let us begin by considering the 'realized' type of eschatology. The most convincing interpretation of this type is found in the writings of Rudolf Bultmann. Modern man, Bultmann thinks, cannot believe in an end of the world in the sense of early Jewish-Christian eschatology. History will continue its course indefinitely, and if it ever does have a termination, this will be due to some natural or man-made cause, not to a divine judgment. The traditional futuristic eschatology is to be regarded as myth. But Bultmann was too much aware of the central place of this myth in New Testament teaching to suppose that it could be simply eliminated. Thus he tries to demythologize it, and believes that he already finds a pointer to such an interpretation in the Gospel of John. 'The meaning in history lies always in the present,' he declares. 'In every moment slumbers the possibility of being the eschatological moment. You must awaken to it.'[10] This eschatological moment is the moment of the ultimate responsible decision of faith. It is also described as the moment in which Jesus Christ is born, suffers, dies and is raised up to eternal life in the soul of the believer.

It is clear that one can go far along these lines toward giving a plausible interpretation of the New Testament theology. Every man is in fact living eschatologically, in the face of an end constituted by his own death. To recognize this is to recapture something of the urgency of those New Testament Christians for whom the time was very short.[11] It is precisely this urgency that seems to be lost when the eschatological events are relegated to the distant future.

Living in the face of death, one is living under judgment as one's unrepeatable acts and decisions give shape to one's life. Here and now, it is possible to taste the quality of 'eternal life', as John's Gospel also seems to teach, for the decisions of faith lead to an integration of the person that raises him above the fleeting and transitory. Equally, of course, it is possible to lose hold of life and to let it be scattered and dissolved in the cares and pleasures of the world. Heaven is not to be conceived as some external reward to be given for good conduct, but rather as the strength and stability of being, generated in the decisions of faith and in the directing of one's life to God. On the other hand, hell is not an arbitrary punishment for sin but simply the dissolution which sin itself produces in the life of the sinner. Though Bultmann himself does not consider the question, the kind of view described would also seem to call for some concept of purgatory, the painful dying to sin and rising with Christ which, in Bultmann's view, is the very essence of the Christian life.

Though we have been considering the eschatological concepts of judgment, eternal life, heaven, hell and purgatory in relation to our present life in this world – and perhaps it is only because we can do this that we can attach meaning to these concepts – it is not therefore implied that judgment, eternal life and the rest can be understood *only* in relation to our present life. Although Bultmann himself is once more silent on the question, there is nothing in principle to prevent us from supposing that the eternal life glimpsed perhaps only momentarily in this world is the beginning of a life that extends beyond death. If it is indeed a life founded on faith and therefore on God, then it is not a life that death could destroy. We may recall, too, our earlier discussion of the resurrection of Jesus, in which we took note of the fact that human life never completes itself within the span of an earthly existence and that man naturally hopes beyond death.[12]

The interpretation of Christian eschatology just considered has many merits, and its insights would certainly need to be brought into any modern account of the matter. It is an interpretation which penetrates into the imagery of the ancient mythology and makes its teaching intelligible and even persuasive. Furthermore, by tying eschatology so firmly to our existence here and now, it prevents the eschatological elements of faith from becoming other-worldly and escapist, as they have so often done. Yet the account is undeniably individualistic, as indeed we were led to expect it would be. This is not altogether a fault. Bultmann stands in the line of Kierkegaard, who rightly valued individual responsibility and commitment as against collective pressures which often become unthinking and unconcerned with the moral evaluation of action. But it remains true that the individual is incomplete apart from his social context, and that an interpretation of eschatology with a strongly individualistic bias, however plausible such an interpretation may be in some respects, is inescapably limited and one-sided. After all, the principal eschatological image of the New Testament is the kingdom of God, and this is an image drawn from the social and political life of man. Certainly, the kingdom of God is more than just the sum of those individuals whose existence has become eschatological through the decision of faith.

So we have to attend also to the voices of those contemporary theologians who are dissatisfied with a realized eschatology, and who insist that the future character of the eschatological events must not be obliterated. We have in mind such theologians as Moltmann and Pannenberg. To be sure, their concern with the future is sometimes exaggerated at the expense of the past and the present, and neither of the thinkers mentioned has succeeded in escaping from mythological ideas which are hard to reconcile with a modern outlook and which introduce considerable obscurity into their theologies. Nevertheless, we can agree with the complaint that if the eschatological events have already occurred or if they are potentialities which may be realized at any time in the lives of individuals, then this would seem to be a good deal less than the kingdom promised in the New Testament. For that kingdom could only be said to have come if, as well as renewed individuals coming into being, there also took place a radical renewal and transformation of the whole social fabric of mankind. The New Testament can speak even of 'a new heaven and a new earth'.[13] This kind of language, and likewise language about a 'new creation' and the 'resurrection of the dead' seems to imply a drastic renovation and reconstitution on a cosmic scale.

Is there any way in which this large-scale futuristic type of eschatology can be made more intelligible, or is it inextricably involved in outworn mythologies and therefore, as Bultmann and many others would hold, not acceptable to modern minds?

We might urge that some of the arguments used in connection with individualized eschatology can be extended. If it is true that no individual human life realizes all its potentialities in its earthly existence, the same is true of any society or community. If there is a fulfilled community, while the way to it undoubtedly lies through history (for there is no other way open to us), that community itself must somehow transcend history. The kingdom of God must somehow transcend history, for this is implicit in the description of it as being 'of God'. Secularized versions of the kingdom which reduce it to an idealized this-worldly society do not take its eschatological character seriously. They fall once more into the errors of nineteenth-century theology and make the kingdom of heaven just another of the illusory utopias that are enthusiastically proclaimed from time to time. Yet to acknowledge the transcendent dimension of the kingdom of God is not to make that kingdom wholly other-worldly or escapist. The way to it, we have insisted, can only lie through the historical. Yet the fulfilment of history, like the fulfilment of the individual human life, would seem to demand a new mode of existence.

Perhaps our attempt to make the notion of the kingdom of God more intelligible to minds suspicious of mythology can be advanced further by another consideration. It has often been pointed out in evolutionary philosophies, from Alexander to Teilhard de Chardin, that the evolutionary process includes not only long stretches of steady uniform development but also some critical leaps when there emerges with relative suddenness something new, something that quite transforms the previously existing state of affairs and marks a breakthrough into a novel mode of being. The emergence of life on earth and, more recently, the emergence of personal beings on earth, are examples of such ontological breakthroughs. There is every reason to expect that there will be further breakthroughs in the future, and the emergence of a radically new type of community, fully personal and fully corporate, might well be among them. I have in mind a community so drastically transformed, so discontinuous with the communities we know now and so transcendent of current utopias, that it could fairly be called eschatological; and yet, as a community recognizably human, personal and fulfilling, it would be in another sense continuous with the communities we know now and already prefigured in that community we call the people of God to the extent that it is striving to manifest the new humanity of Christ. For the next breakthrough – if there is to be one – will be different from all that have gone before, for it will require the conscious coworking of the creatures with the Creator.

In the last paragraphs, we have inevitably become more speculative, for the future is a mystery. But the ground of our hope is not speculative. It rests on the fact that in Christ and his people we have seen the hidden glory. And having seen that glory, the people cannot rest but presses forward to the goal when the glory will be manifested through the whole creation, 'when men will come from east and west, and from north and south, and sit at table in the kingdom of God'.[14]

Notes

1. See above, p.20.
2. Matthew 16.18.
3. See above, p.24.
4. See above, p.55.
5. I Thessalonians 4.13-18.
6. Johannes Weiss, *Jesus' Proclamation of the Kingdom of God*, tr. R. H. Hiers and D. L. Holland, London: SCM Press, 1971, pp.131,135.

7. See above, p.24.
8. II Peter 3.3-4.
9. John 12.31.
10. Rudolph Bultmann, *History and Eschatology*, Edinburgh: Edinburgh University Press, 1957, p.155.

11. I Corinthians 7.29.
12. See above, p.63.

13. Revelation 21.1.
14. Luke 13.29.

A Guide to Further Reading

The reader of this book who wishes to pursue the study of theology further would do well to read next one or more of the larger modern systematic treatments of Christian theology. The following books are all fairly detailed works and represent different approaches: Gustav Aulen, *The Faith of the Christian Church*, SCM Press, London, 1954; Regin Prenter, *Creation and Redemption*, Fortress Press, Philadelphia, 1967; Oliver C. Quick, *Doctrines of the Creed*, Nisbet, London, 1938, John Macquarrie, *Principles of Christian Theology*, SCM Press, London, 1966; Gordon D. Kaufman, *Systematic Theology: A Historicist Perspective*, Scribner, New York, 1968; Ludwig Ott, *Fundamentals of Catholic Dogma*, Mercier Press, Cork, 1958. Mention should also be made of the so-called 'Dutch Catechism' – *A New Catechism: Catholic Faith for Adults*, prepared by the Nijmegen Higher Catechetical Institute, Burns & Oakes, London, 1967. On a much larger scale than any of the books listed so far are two major achievements of twentieth-century theology – Karl Barth's *Church Dogmatics*, T. & T. Clark, Edinburgh, 1936 onward, and Paul Tillich's *Systematic Theology*, Nisbet, London, 1953 onward. Barth's work consists of four volumes, each divided into several substantial part-volumes, while Tillich's work comprises three volumes. These vast works are not for beginners, but parts of them may be read to make acquaintance with these two giants of modern theology and their widely different approaches.

Men (and some women) have been writing Christian theology for nearly two thousand years and no contemporary theologians (even those who are deliberately trying to break with the past) can remain uninfluenced by the tradition or be intelligible apart from some knowledge of it. Useful introductions to this tradition are provided by such books as A. D. Galloway, *Basic*

Readings in Theology, Allen & Unwin, London, 1964 and Hugh T. Kerr, *Readings in Christian Thought*, Abingdon Press, Nashville, 1966. Both books contain selections from the early centuries down to modern times, and there are helpful notes.

From reading selections, one might go on to study in more detail some of the great classics of Christian theology. I have in mind especially those major theological systems which became influential for subsequent theology. St Thomas Aquinas' *Summa Theologiae*, written between 1265 and 1274, is so vast that it could occupy a lifetime of study, but some parts of it have to be read if one is to understand discussions that have gone on ever since – e.g., his famous 'five ways' of demonstrating the existence of God have remained important for all subsequent arguments over natural theology and theism. The best edition of the *Summa*, containing Latin text, English translation and copious notes, is under the general editorship of Thomas Gilby, OP, Eyre and Spottiswoode, London, 1964 onward. *The Existence and Nature of God* is treated in the second of the sixty volumes in this edition. The greatest theological achievement of the Reformation was John Calvin's *Institutes of the Christian Religion*. The first Latin edition appeared in 1536, and Calvin continued to revise and expand it until 1560. The best English edition is the one edited by J. T. McNeill, SCM Press, London, 1960. The father of modern theology, Friedrich Schleiermacher, taught that experience is the principal source for theological reflection; his major work is *The Christian Faith*, German original, 1821; English translation, T. & T. Clark, Edinburgh, 1928. Almost equally important was the work of another nineteenth-century German theologian, Albrecht Ritschl. Stressing the ethical and corporate dimensions of Christianity, his influence was important for the 'Social Gospel'. His theology found systematic expression in *Justification and Reconciliation*, German original, 1874; English translation, T. & T. Clark, Edinburgh, 1900.

When we turn from complete theologies to books dealing with special topics, it is appropriate to begin with the notion of the people of God, since this has played such a large part in the present book. The idea of the people of God was prominent in the thinking of the Second Vatican Council, whose teaching may be studied in *The Documents of Vatican II*, ed. Walter M.

Abbott, SJ, Herder & Herder, New York, 1966. The people of
God *motif* has been dominant in theological thinking about the
church in recent years, and not only in Roman Catholic
thinkers. It is beautifully expounded in what is perhaps the
best book to have been written on the church for a very long
time, Louis Bouyer's *L'Eglise de Dieu*, Cerf, Paris, 1970; not yet
translated into English. Other works are Hans Küng's *The
Church*, Burns & Oates, London, 1967, and, stressing the missionary role of the people of God, Colin Williams' *The Church*,
Lutterworth Press, London, 1968. One should not overlook the
writings of John Knox who, for a long time, has been stressing
the corporate nature of the church in such books as *The Early
Church and the Coming Great Church*, Epworth Press, London,
1957.

The concept of revelation has been much discussed in recent
theology. Among the best books on the subject are H. Richard
Niebuhr, *The Meaning of Revelation*, Macmillan, New York,
1941, and Gabriel Moran, FSC, *Theology of Revelation*, Burns
& Oates, London, 1966. A critical and historical analysis of the
different theories of revelation is contained in Avery Dulles, SJ,
Revelation Theology: A History, Burns & Oates, London, 1969.
The Christian idea of revelation implies an understanding of
history as the bearer of revelation, so that there have also been
many theological studies of the nature of history. Among them
may be mentioned Hans Urs von Balthasar, *A Theology of
History*, Sheed & Ward, London, 1963.

There are many excellent books on the doctrine of man. Still
important is Reinhold Niebuhr's massive work, *The Nature and
Destiny of Man*, Nisbet, Welwyn, 1941: as is likewise Martin
Buber's little classic, *I and Thou*, revised edition, T. & T. Clark,
Edinburgh, 1957. Abraham Heschel, *Who Is Man?*, Stanford
University Press, Stanford, 1965, and Roger L. Shinn, *Man – the
New Humanism*, Westminster Press, Philadelphia, 1968, are
both important studies. In this area one should not neglect the
work of secular writers, such as Albert Camus' brilliant book,
The Rebel: An Essay on Man in Revolt, Penguin Books, Lon-
don, 1969.

While there is a plethora of books on man, there is a great
scarcity of books on the theology of nature, and this neglect
may be symptomatic of our present environmental crisis. Pierre

Teilhard de Chardin writes of the theological significance of the material world in *The Divine Milieu*, Collins, London, 1960, John Cobb has related Christian theology to Whitehead's organic view of nature in *A Christian Natural Theology*, Lutterworth Press, London, 1967. Recent books on science and religion may also be consulted, e.g., John Habgood, *Religion and Science*, Mills and Boon, London, 1959, and Eric Rust, *Science and Faith*, Oxford University Press, New York, 1967.

There are many books (including many up-to-date books) on the doctrine of God, and this would seem to show that interest in this particular topic is greater than is sometimes supposed. We can only list some titles: Eric L. Mascall, *He Who Is*, revised edition, Darton, Longman & Todd, London, 1966; Schubert M. Ogden, *The Reality of God*, SCM Press, London, 1966; John Macquarrie, *God-Talk*, SCM Press, London, 1967; John A. T. Robinson, *Exploration into God*, SCM Press, London, 1967; Fritz Buri, *How Can We Still Speak Responsibly of God?*, Fortress Press, Philadelphia, 1968; Langdon Gilkey, *Naming the Whirlwind: The Renewal of God-Language*, Bobbs-Merrill, Indianapolis, 1969; Ronald Gregor Smith, *The Doctrine of God*, Collins, London, 1970.

Christology is another field with an extensive literature. The problems are seen differently nowadays because of the results of historical criticism of the New Testament and the determination of theologians to take more seriously the genuine humanity of Christ. Important books include: Rudolf Bultmann, *Jesus Christ and Mythology*, SCM Press, London, 1958; Dietrich Bonhoeffer, *Christology*, Collins, London, 1966; Wolfhart Pannenberg, *Jesus – God and Man*, SCM Press, London, 1968. There is an important essay by Karl Rahner, SJ, on 'Current Problems of Christology' in the first volume of his *Theological Investigations*, Darton, Longman & Todd, London, 1961.

When we come to the doctrine of the Holy Spirit, we strike once more on a neglected area. George S. Hendry, *The Holy Spirit in Christian Theology*, revised edition, SCM Press, London, 1965, and Dale Moody, *Spirit of the Living God*, Westminster Press, Philadelphia, 1968, may be consulted. The Christian life, which we have discussed in the same chapter as the Holy Spirit, has received more attention from theologians. Hans Küng's *Justification*, Burns & Oates, London, 1964, and

Daniel D. Williams' *The Spirit and Forms of Love*, Harper &
Row, New York, 1968, are outstanding books of recent years.

On the sacraments, Oliver C. Quick affords a general introduction in his book, *The Christian Sacraments*, Nisbet, London,
1927. The literature on the eucharist is especially rich. Joachim
Jeremias, *The Eucharistic Words of Jesus*, SCM Press, London,
1966, is unsurpassed as a study of origins. Gregory Dix, OSB,
has given a fascinating account of the development of the rite in
The Shape of the Liturgy, Dacre Press, London, 1945. New
trends in eucharistic theology are discussed by Joseph Powers,
SJ, in *Eucharistic Theology*, Burns & Oates, London, 1968.
Since the word and sacraments go together as vehicles of the
people's life, this is an appropriate place to note books on the
position and authority of the Bible today. We mention two:
Alonso Schökel, SJ, *The Inspired Word*, Herder & Herder, New
York, 1965, and Robert H. Bryant, *The Bible's Authority To-
day*, Augsburg Press, Minneapolis, 1968.

The subjects of ministry and mission are adequately discussed in the books on the church, already mentioned. But one
classic that is still germane to current discussions should be
added, R. C. Moberly's *Ministerial Priesthood*, Murray, London, 1910, frequently reprinted.

Interest in prayer has been reviving. A very good introduction
to this subject is the book of Mark Gibbard, SSJE, *Why Pray?*,
SCM Press, London, 1970. Other works are Martin Thornton's
Prayer: A New Encounter, Hodder & Stoughton, London, 1972,
and John Macquarrie's *Paths in Spirituality*, SCM Press, London, 1972.

The biblical background of eschatology was interpreted by
R. H. Charles in a well-kown book, *Eschatology: A Critical
History*, new edition, Schocken Books, New York, 1963. Johannes
Weiss' notable book, which was first published in Germany in
1892 and marked the beginning of the new interest in eschatology, has at last been translated into English as *Jesus' Proclamation of the Kingdom of God*, SCM Press, London, 1971.
The two opposing contemporary interpretations of eschatology
mentioned in our chapter on this topic may be conveniently
studied in Rudolf Bultmann's *History and Eschatology*, Edinburgh University Press, Edinburgh, 1957, and Jürgen Moltmann's *Theology of Hope*, SCM Press, London, 1967.

Index

Index